THE SPICY CAMP COOKBOOK

The
Spicy
Camp Cookbook

M. Timothy O'Keefe

Copyright © 1997 by M. Timothy O'Keefe
Printed in the United States of America
All Rights Reserved
Published by Menasha Ridge Press
First edition, first printing

Cover design by Grant Tatum.
Interior design by Kandace Hawkinson.
Illustrations by Dorene Davis.

Library of Congress Cataloging-in-Publication Data

O'Keefe, M. Timothy
      The spicy camp cookbook / by M. Timothy O'Keefe.
            p.   cm.
      Includes index.
      ISBN 0-89732-188-X
      1. Outdoor cookery.   2. Spices.   3. Title
TX823.0427 1996   96-48481
641.5'78--dc21
                                              CIP

Menasha Ridge Press
700 South 28th Street, Suite 206
Birmingham, AL 35233
(800) 247-9437
http://www.menasharidge.com

Dedication

To Christine Donovan, one of the best cooks I've
ever met, who helped prepare, sample, and improve
much of what follows. And to Butch Tatro, Jeff
Butler, Clint Putnal, and Norman Jeeter for all the
outdoor cooking tips I picked up from you during
our decades of camping together.

HOW TO USE THIS BOOK

Measures for each recipe are American. The appendix provides an equivalent-measure and conversion chart that also includes British measures.

Advisory: Some scientist at some point has declared every item of food and every method of cooking in this book to be hazardous to your health. Therefore, taking current science to its ultimate absurdity, eating can only kill you. The alternative, however, is not nearly as satisfying or fulfilling, and the end result is the same. Personally, I intend to eat and drink until the day I die. You, however, must decide your own course—and may your courses be many.

CONTENTS

Why You Need
Spice in Your Life

Today, people are more interested in cooking with spices and herbs than ever before. Go to the spice aisle in almost any large supermarket and you'll see spices that once were found only in small ethnic grocery stores.

For instance, both a Szechuan-style pepper blend and a dry jerk seasoning (used in Caribbean cooking) have recently been introduced by McCormick & Co., one of the nation's oldest spice suppliers. Other companies have added dozens of new steak and chicken seasonings, most of them intended to be used in outdoor cooking.

Because so many of the newly introduced seasonings pack something of a bite, many people mistakenly assume that spices also make foods hot-tasting. Not true. Spices and herbs add many new and wonderful flavors, but they normally do not make something hot-tasting. Spices and herbs are not like hot sauces, which tend to be so overpowering that all you taste is the hot sauce itself.

It is the combination of spices in the right variety and amount that makes each dish unique and distinctive in every five-star restaurant. However, spices and herbs can be blended with chilies and peppers to produce dishes that are quite hot, as the Chinese, Mexican, and Caribbean recipes in this book amply illustrate. Those of you who enjoy trying new things will be happy to discover that a good Jamaican jerk seasoning will hold its own against Szechuan-style peppers any day. And that the much-maligned curry powder is not normally hot, but flavorful instead. It's the added chilies that make some Indian curries so tasty hot.

The growing popularity of curry is astounding, even in regions traditionally known for an appetite limited to meat and potatoes. Whoever would have expected that a poll conducted in 1996 would show that curry was Britain's most popular food?

The recipes in *The Spicy Camp Cookbook* come from all over the world. I have been fortunate enough to dine on all seven continents, although eating outdoors on a cold Antarctic day was limited to half a chocolate candy bar and half a bottle of champagne—still pretty gourmet, considering the circumstances.

Eating around the world, I realized that one of the best souvenirs from a trip was a recipe of the best meal I had. Just because I was leaving a country didn't mean I had to leave behind its cuisine—with one exception: You'll not find any penguin or seal recipes from Antarctica, or any other recipe that calls for any sort of meat, fruit, or vegetable that is unusual or hard to find. After all, foods themselves are rarely exotic: It's the spices and herbs used to season them that create the extraordinary aromas and flavors.

In many countries, cooking is routinely done outdoors with grills or ovens, so it seems only natural that these recipes be adapted for camping, which is being interpreted in the broadest possible sense. Self-contained backpackers, tenters and river runners with ice chests, RV owners with all the conveniences, yachties and boaters with well-stocked ship's galleys, and apartment and home dwellers who simply like to cook outdoors should all find plenty of worthwhile recipes. To help you locate recipes according to your cooking circumstances, most have been grouped according to how they're most easily prepared: grill, skillet or oven.

The following recipes not only were collected or adapted by me but also came from friends, family, and sources that I can no longer specifically remember. Because you make quite an investment when you purchase a cookbook (the price of the book is insignificant compared to the cost of the food you prepare), all of the recipes have been thoroughly tested.

Of course, some of our tastes may differ, but I promise you this: There isn't a boring or a just "okay" recipe in the bunch. There certainly isn't a bad one. Recipes of that sort were discarded, along with the food they destroyed, on more than one occasion.

For the most part, these dishes are right in line with today's emphasis on eating smart. Sour cream, butter, rich cheeses, thick gravies, and triple-stacked cheeseburgers taste so good because they are so loaded with fat. But when you have spices providing a flavor that is just as rich, you usually don't miss the fat, so fats have been reduced or eliminated wherever possible. Still, this is hardly a fat-free cookbook. Olive or canola oil is used in many dishes.

Overall, the goal of *The Spicy Camp Cookbook* is to supply you with meals that are so appetizing and so memorable that you will want to make many of them over and over again in the years ahead. Some of these recipes I fix regularly whether I'm camping or at home because I think their taste is hard to beat. If you like even a handful of recipes just as much—and I can almost guarantee that you will—then this book will have served its purpose.

Not only will it have added pleasure to your life, it will also have made it spicier.

CHAPTER ONE

The Spices

A ROLL CALL

This chapter features descriptions of the spices most frequently used throughout the book. As you'll note, almost none originated in this part of the world, though some of the trees and shrubs are now grown in warmer climates almost everywhere. The term "spice" is being used liberally. Technically, a spice is made only from seeds, kernels, fruits, roots, rootstocks, berries, bark, or flower buds. However, herbs and aromatic plants are also commonly called spices, so everything used for seasoning (including commercial preparations like soy sauce) is being lumped into the spice category. We are more interested in the right flavoring than the proper taxonomy.

Another important note: The taste of some spices, such as ginger and nutmeg, is so sublime in small amounts that it's often tempting to double or even triple the suggested amount so a dish will be twice as good. It normally doesn't work that way. Too much spice is often worse than no spice at all.

Allspice: A berry from the West Indian pimiento tree that seems to have the flavors of several spices, particularly cinnamon and cloves. Sometimes called the Jamaica pepper, this is an important ingredient in Jamaican jerk seasonings.

Arrowroot: This tropical American plant, so named because it was once used to treat wounds from poison arrows, is used mostly for thickening sauces.

Basil: There are many different varieties, but sweet basil is the one used in Italian cooking or anytime piquancy is needed for soups or salads. Basil, a member of the mint family, was originally a Near Eastern herb.

Bay Leaf: This is the leaf of the laurel, a tree and shrub originally grown in the Mediterranean. Bay leaf is used to flavor meat and seafood dishes.

Bell Pepper: Also called the sweet pepper.

Capers: Dried and pickled capers add pungency. Capers are the bud of the caper bush, found in Central Asia and the Mediterranean.

Cardamom: A member of the ginger family, cardamom is used in Indian cooking for its sweet pungency.

Cayenne Pepper: Also called red pepper, it is ground into a red powder to enliven meat dishes and sauces. It should be used sparingly.

Chili Powder: Created in the American Southwest to imitate Tex-Mex cooking, it is most often a blend of chili pepper, cumin, oregano, and garlic. Cloves and allspice are sometimes added.

Chili Sauce: Used mostly as a condiment or in a marinade, this sauce is thick like catsup and usually contains tomatoes, green peppers, sugar, onion, vinegar, and other spices.

Chive: The leaves of this herb supply a mild onion flavor.

Cinnamon: One of the world's most popular spices. Sweet, pungent, and very aromatic, it is made from the bark of any of several trees. Traditionally, most cinnamon used in the United States is from cassia bark, technically considered a cinnamon substitute. The cassia is a tree native to China.

Clove: The pungent bud of the clove tree, it provides a warm, spicy flavor. Oil of clove should be used much more sparingly. Whole cloves can be turned into ground cloves with the aid of a hammer.

Cooking Wine: Never to be used in a recipe calling for wine. Cooking wines generally are inferior wines with salt added. Once the alcohol evaporates, all that is left is the flavor of the wine. An inherently bad wine cannot add anything but a degraded taste.

Coriander: A member of the parsley family used in salads, soups, and stews and highly favored in India, Mexico, and the Caribbean, places where people really know how to spice up their food.

Cumin: Also spelled "cummin" or called by its Italian name, "comino," this nutty-flavored herb is related to parsley. Native to Egypt, it is an ingredient in curry and chili powders.

Curry Powder: Actually a form of condiment that is a blend of pungent spices, including cumin, coriander, cayenne, fenugreek, and turmeric. Other ingredients that are sometimes added include cassia, allspice, cloves, ginger, mace, mustard, fennel, and black or white pepper. In some countries, the curry powder is made fresh for every meal.

Dijon Mustard: Originally made in Dijon, France, this mild mustard includes white wine, vinegar, and other spices.

Dill: A member of the parsley family, most often used to enliven the flavor of fish dishes.

Dry Mustard: Mustard seed that has been ground into a powder. It can be used as a seasoning like pepper.

Fennel: Yet another member of the parsley family, this one supplies a licorice taste.

Filé: Never actually mentioned in this book, but something you need to know about in case you become inspired enough to experiment more. Very popular in Creole cooking, filé is simply dried young sassafras leaves that have been ground into a powder to thicken soups and stews. Sassafras is also commonly made into tea and used in perfumes. Filé gumbo is perhaps the best-known dish.

Garlic: Clearly a gift from the gods, the head (or bulb) of the garlic plant has a distinctive taste. Minced garlic is usually stored in jars in garlic oil. Garlic powder is stronger in flavor than garlic salt.

Ginger: Ground ginger is far more potent than grated or sliced ginger root. When substituting ground ginger for grated or sliced, use only half as much. Europeans and Americans tend to use ground ginger in their cooking.

Hoisin Sauce: Popular in Asian cooking, this thick sauce is made up of soybeans, garlic, and other spices. Also sometimes called Peking sauce.

Horseradish: A very pungent root. Prepared horseradish is mostly just the grated root, while horseradish sauce contains a mixture of other items. In cooking, only the prepared horseradish is recommended.

Jamaica Pepper: The same thing as allspice.

Jerk: The hot, spicy seasonings used in Jamaican barbecuing. Allspice is an important ingredient.

Mace: The red membrane between the husk and fruit of the nutmeg tree. Tastes like nutmeg but stronger.

Marjoram: A member of the mint family that supplies a sweet, tangy taste to meats. Wild marjoram is the same thing as oregano.

Molasses: A thick syrup made from sugar in the refining process.

Nutmeg: Comes from the same tree as mace, but nutmeg is sweeter. Nutmeg can be very pungent when used with a heavy hand.

Olives: A rich, oily fruit. Unripe olives are green and pickled in brine. Most ripe olives are black, though some are green. Black olives are milder-tasting because they are not pickled in as salty a brine as unripe olives.

Onions: Another flavorful, pungent gift from the gods. There are two types: The young ones are called green scallions, while the mature onions are the dried white, yellow, and red bulbs found in most grocery stores. This herb is actually a member of the lily family.

Onion Powder: Pure onion in powder form that may be substituted for onion bulbs in cooking.

Onion Salt: Common table salt mixed with onion powder.

Oregano: A member of the mint family, it has more of a bite than marjoram. Very popular in Italian cooking.

Paprika: Made from a red pepper than can be mild or quite hot. Most associated with Hungarian cooking, paprika is used both for flavor and for decoration.

Parmesan: A sharp, grated cheese made from skim milk.

Parsley: There are many varieties, but the most popular is probably Italian parsley. Used as both a seasoning and a decoration, fresh parsley has a rich, pungent flavor.

Pepper: A pungent seasoning made from dry, immature berries. Black pepper is derived from such berries, called peppercorns. White pepper, which is milder, is made by removing the shell of the mature berries and grinding the white seeds inside.

Rosemary: A shrub of the mint family with leaves shaped like pine needles. Very pungent, and can be overpowering if too much is used. Fresh rosemary is normally chopped. Dry rosemary is often crushed and simmered in water to obtain the maximum flavor.

Sage: A slightly bitter member of the mint family, used for seasoning meats and marinades, best known for ruining turkey stuffing when overused.

Seasoned Salt: Plain old table salt that has been modified with onion, garlic, and similar flavor enhancers.

Soy Sauce: Of Asian origin, this dark sauce includes soybean extracts, wheat, and yeast in addition to incredible amounts of salt.

Tabasco Pepper: A very hot, pungent pepper named after Tabasco, a state in Mexico. Tabasco Sauce is a commercially sold, trademarked hot pepper sauce.

Thyme: A shrub related to the mint family that supplies a warm, somewhat pungent aroma.

Turmeric: The root of a plant related to the ginger family, turmeric is an important flavoring that gives the yellow color to prepared mustard and curry powder.

Vinegar: Apple cider vinegar is gold in color and has the aroma of apples. Wine vinegar, more common to Europe, is more acidic than apple cider vinegar.

QUICK SUBSTITUTIONS

Sometimes it's just not possible to have everything you need on hand, either because of transporting problems or because you realize at the last minute that you've forgotten something. Here are some substitutions that work quite well:

Liquid egg substitute, 1/2 cup = 2 eggs
Prepared mustard, 1 Tbl = 1 Tbl dry mustard and 1 Tbl white wine or vinegar
Dry mustard, 1 Tbl = 3 Tbl prepared mustard
Onion, 1 medium chopped = 1 Tbl minced onion, reconstituted
Soy sauce, 1/4 cup = 3 Tbl Worcestershire and 1 Tbl water
Wine for marinades only, 1/2 cup = 1/4 cup vinegar plus 1/4 cup of water plus 1 Tbl sugar
Tomato paste, 1 Tbl = 1 Tbl catsup

COOKING OILS

Wherever possible, the recipes use monounsaturated oils instead of butter or margarine. The most recommended is olive oil, although canola and peanut oil are also monounsaturated. However, current medical research shows that people who consume large amounts of olive oil—even when they eat lots of other fats—tend to have fewer heart problems.

Olive oil is available in many different grades. Olive oil is graded according to its acidity and how it was pressed.

Light Olive Oil: This is the best for frying, since it has the highest smoke point. Light olive oil goes through a filtration process that produces an oil that is lighter in color, flavor, and aroma. It is also good for baking and any other cooking where the normal taste of olive is not desired.

Extra Virgin: This comes from the first press, a cold press; it has the lowest acidity and is the most expensive. Best used in cold dishes or added to foods after cooking, since it loses both its flavor and its aroma when heated.

Virgin Olive Oil: Also a first-press oil, but with a higher acidity level, ranging from 1 to 3 percent.

Fine Olive Oil: A blend of extra virgin and virgin olive oils.

Olive Oil: Sometimes called pure olive oil. Often the least expensive and with a high acidity rating (over 3.3%). This is a blend of either extra virgin or virgin olive oil and refined olive oil.

Olive oil can be stored in a refrigerator for up to a year, and in a cool, dark place for about six months. Olive oil does become cloudy when refrigerated but regains its natural gold color once it's at room temperature.

CHAPTER TWO

Transporting and Menu Planning

RECIPES KEYED FOR YOUR SITUATION

Whether you're backpacking, river running, tenting, RVing, or boating/ yachting, there are many good recipes here just for you. The recipes vary considerably in their complexity and their need for refrigeration. To help you determine at a glance which are best suited for a particular activity, some of the recipes are accompanied by a symbol. The symbol 🐾 indicates that the recipe is suitable for those without refrigeration. However, people in cool climates should have no real trouble packing in a few vegetables, spices, and even desserts. Also, where fresh chicken is called for, people without refrigeration may substitute canned chicken.

ICE CHEST BASICS

With a good ice supply, virtually anything—meat, dairy products, and the like—can be safely stored for a three-day weekend trip and even longer. Yogurt and sour cream can last in an ice chest for as long as a week. You can do several things to make your ice last as long as possible.

* Chill everything before leaving home. Warm soft drinks, water bottles, and so on will use up your ice in no time.

* For extended trips and/or camping in hot weather, freeze fresh meat in freezer paper. Then, before starting your trip, place the wrapped frozen meat in a resealable plastic freezer bag. Not only will the plastic bag keep the meat fresher longer, but the freezer bags will also protect the meat once the ice starts to melt, and you'll be able to use the resealable bags for marinades.

* Block ice lasts far longer than crushed ice. You can make crushed ice last longer by leaving it in the bag.

* You can make your own block ice by filling plastic gallon milk containers with water and freezing them. When the ice in the jugs melts, you'll have refreshing cold water to drink or extra water for cooking.

* When space permits, carry two ice chests of different sizes. Put your soft drinks, cold water bottles, and other items that campers will be after frequently in the larger chest. In the smaller chest, which is to be opened once or twice a day and then only briefly, place the most perishable items, such as meats and dairy products.

* Ice chests should be off-limits to young children, who have a tendency to dawdle or not put the lid back on tightly. Have the kids come to you if they need a drink. Of course, you'll need to arrange the drinks in the chest yourself so you'll be able to find various items quickly.

* Items last longer when an ice chest is tightly packed with ice and frozen foods.

* Since warm air rises and cold air seeks the lowest point, place ice on both the top and bottom of the cooler.

* Once your ice starts to melt, drain the melt water from the frozen food chest and use it for cooking or drinking or whatever. Because the melt water is above freezing, it causes ice to thaw faster.

* However, cool melt water is colder than the air inside an ice chest. After the ice starts melting significantly in your drink chest, keep the melt water but place the ice bag(s) on top of the drinks.

* Always keep your ice chest shaded.

ADVANCE PREPARATION

The marinades

Some of the marinades require only a few ingredients and can be made at camp. Others call for a host of ingredients, probably more than you want to lug with you. Those should be made at home a day or two before you leave.

The easiest way to prepare a marinade is to put everything in a resealable freezer bag. Quart-sized freezer bags will handle stew meat, chicken breasts, and fish fillets, but you'll need larger ones for whole chickens, chicken legs, and spare ribs.

After combining all the marinade ingredients in a freezer bag, add the meat and chill the bag in the refrigerator overnight. That way, when you reach your campsite, the marinating will be complete and all you'll need to add is fire for cooking.

If you're going on an extended trip or you fear the marinade will make the meat too mushy for your liking, freeze it instead of chilling it. That way the meat won't be marinating the entire trip, only after it begins to thaw.

12

On occasions when preparations get put off to the last minute and the meat you want to marinate is still frozen, prepare the marinade in a resealable plastic bag. You can add the meat to the marinade after it starts thawing or on the morning you intend to prepare it for dinner.

SAMPLE MENUS

The majority of camping trips last just three to four days. Following are some sample menus using the book's recipes. It's always a good idea to test any recipe at home first in case you want to make any adjustments that might better suit your tastes.

Backpacker's Menu
Most of these recipes are for two to four people, so the weight of the canned items can be distributed around. The breakfast recipes would use powdered eggs. The trail mixes and some other ingredients should be prepared ahead of time.

Day 1
Lunch: Spicy Chicken Stir Fry *(Chapter 8)*
Snack: Fruit Cocktail Trail Mix *(Chapter 14)*
Dinner: Chicken Fajitas or Chicken Tostadas *(Chapter 8)*

Day 2
Breakfast: Pepperoni Egg Pizza *(Chapter 5)*
Lunch: Curried Chicken *(Chapter 8)*
Snack: Chilies, Cheese, and Ham *(Chapter 7)*
Dinner: Easy Gumbo *(Chapter 9)*

Day 3
Breakfast: Eggs, Cheese and Ham Ole *(Chapter 5)*
Lunch: Blackened Tuna over Pasta *(Chapter 12)*
Snack: Caribbean Crunch Trail Mix *(Chapter 14)*
Dinner: Chicken and Radish Stir Fry *(Chapter 8)*

Day 4
Breakfast: Huevos Rancheros *(Chapter 5)*
Lunch: Ham and Pineapple Curry *(Chapter 5)*
Snack: Classic Gorp Trail Mix *(Chapter 14)*
Dinner: Spicy Shrimp with Angel Hair Pasta *(Chapter 12)*

Camping with an Ice Chest

Don't overlook the simple and easy backpacking recipes. A few are repeated here as a reminder.

Day 1
Lunch: Hot-n-Spicy Cheeseburgers *(Chapter 11)*
Appetizer/Soup: French Onion Soup *(Chapter 9)*
Dinner: London Broil with Mustard Marinade *(Chapter 11)*
Horseradish Beets or Saucy Corn *(Chapter 6)*
Dessert: Cherry No-Fat Cheesecake *(Chapter 14)*

Day 2
Breakfast: Spicy Leftover Steak *(Chapter 5)*
Basil Potatoes *(Chapter 5)*
Lunch: Chicken Fajitas *(Chapter 8)*
Appetizer/Soup: Apple and Bread Soup *(Chapter 9)*
Dinner: Grilled Jerk Chicken *(Chapter 11)*
Curried Corn or Quick BBQ Beans *(Chapter 6)*
Dessert: Bananas and Oats *(Chapter 14)*

Day 3
Breakfast: Pepperoni Egg Pizza *(Chapter 5)*
Lunch: BBQ Chicken Stir Fry *(Chapter 8)* or
Greek-Style Spaghetti *(Chapter 12)* with Easy Garlic Bread *(Chapter 14)*
Appetizer/Soup: Baba Ghanoush or
Artichoke Hearts with Roquefort Dressing *(Chapter 7)*
Dinner: Beef Peanut Stew *(Chapter 9)* or Chinese-Style Ribs *(Chapter 11)*
Spicy Vegetables in Foil or Broccoli with Herbs *(Chapter 6)*
Dessert: Leftover Cherry No-Fat Cheesecake *(Chapter 14)*

Day 4
Breakfast: Jamaican Rum Toast *(Chapter 5)*
Banana Fritters *(Chapter 14)*
Lunch: Lemon Fried Chicken *(Chapter 8)*
or Classic Shish Kebabs *(Chapter 11)*
Appetizer/Soups: Anchovy Dip *(Chapter 7)*
Dinner: Grilled Onions *(Chapter 6)*
Fresh Tomatoes Oregano *(Chapter 6)*
Curry and Honey-Glazed Chicken *(Chapter 11)*
Dessert: Spicy Popcorn *(Chapter 14)*

Camping Deluxe (with real refrigeration and storage)
These menus have more elaborate combinations that may require two cooking methods, such as a grill and an oven, or a stove burner and an oven. These recipes taste just as good at home as they do away from it.

Day 1
Lunch: Greek-Style Spaghetti *(Chapter 12)* with Easy Garlic Bread *(Chapter 14)*
Appetizer/Soup: Chilies con Queso *(Chapter 7)*
Dinner: Indian-Style Marinated Chicken *(Chapter 11)*
Nutty Broccoli and Cauliflower *(Chapter 6)*
Dessert: Key Lime Pie *(Chapter 14)*

Day 2
Breakfast: Flank Steak Diablo *(Chapter 5)*
Basil Potatoes *(Chapter 5)*
Lunch: Caesar Salad with Blackened Chicken
or Mock Lobster Salad with Ginger *(Chapter 10)*
Appetizer/Soup: Herb Spread *(Chapter 7)*
Dinner: Curried Chicken Noodle Soup *(Chapter 9)*
Easy Garlic Bread *(Chapter 14)*
Dessert: Sinfully Rich No-Fat Chocolate Swirl Cheesecake *(Chapter 14)*

Day 3
Breakfast: Berries-n-Cream *(Chapter 5)*
Eggs Benedict with Smoked Turkey *(Chapter 5)*
Lunch: Hungarian Goulash Soup *(Chapter 9)*
Appetizer/Soup: Greek-Style Meatballs *(Chapter 7)*
Dinner: Honey-Mustard Fish or Spicy Steamed Whole Fish *(Chapter 12)*
Spicy Roasted Potatoes *(Chapter 6)*
Broccoli with Herbs *(Chapter 6)*
Dessert: Leftover Key Lime Pie *(Chapter 14)*

Day 4
Breakfast: Spicy Potato Pancakes *(Chapter 5)*
The Perfect Omelette *(Chapter 5)*
Lunch: Avocado Pasta *(Chapter 6)* or Spicy/Hot Salmon Burgers *(Chapter 12)*
Appetizer/Soup: Shrimp Cocktail *(Chapter 7)*
Dinner: Lemon Fried Chicken *(Chapter 8)* or
Chicken and Cranberries *(Chapter 13)*
Spicy Spinach *(Chapter 6)*
Dessert: Leftover Chocolate Swirl Cheesecake *(Chapter 14)*

BUYING AND PACKING FOODS

Because I use many spices regularly, I find that I save quite a bit of money by buying them in large containers at a warehouse store like Sam's Club or Price/Costco. For instance, I can purchase a year's supply worth of oregano for what a supermarket charges for just a few ounces. Small ethnic groceries often have the best selection and variety of spices.

I transfer any spice that comes in a plastic container to a glass jar with a screw-on lid. I find that glass jars store things better and keep them much fresher far longer than plastic. But when it comes to transporting the spices on camping trips, I transfer a small amount of each spice to a resealable plastic bag or a small plastic bottle with a screw-on cap. In cool weather, I transport even perishable items like minced garlic this way.

When I'm canoeing, boating, or tent camping and refrigeration is no problem, I like to cook the meal for the first night at home, since time sometimes gets all-too-compressed that first day out. One of the best ways to transport such meals is in resealable plastic bags that you can just place in a pot of boiling water to heat up. No cooking mess, no cleanup afterward.

Realizing that even the best resealable plastic bag will sometimes fail and leak all over an ice chest or backpack, a good investment is the Seal-Meal, a device that has been around for years. When it seals a plastic container, the container stays sealed. This is a good method not only for transporting vegetables but also for sealing dry drink mixes in the right amount for your drink container. One of the easiest ways to do this is by using and sealing the liners intended for baby bottles.

Packaged Mixes

There are lots of good packaged mixes that are almost impossible to improve upon, and from a camper's point of view, it would be absurd to try. When you don't have the means to carry or refrigerate items, by all means use the packaged mixes. I certainly do. Unfortunately, many of the freeze-dried mixes made for campers have all the taste excitement of baby food. But after you use some of the following recipes, you will know how adding the right spices can sometimes perform miracles.

Zatarain's makes several good Cajun-style mixes, such as dirty rice and red beans and rice. You can make a complete meal from either by just adding a can of chicken, turkey, or tuna. But look at the labels on Zatarain's and all other mixes. The salt content may surprise you. Some mixes also contain the flavor enhancer MSG, to which many people, including me, are allergic. Yet I don't find the MSG levels in Zatarain's to be a problem, though others may.

A Taste of Thai is another brand that has some interesting mixes, though I found them too bland compared to the real thing in Thailand. But you can easily spice things up with ginger, chilies, and the like.

Never overlook some of the easy but dramatic variations that a small packet of spices can make to the simplest meal. For instance, if you're planning to fix just burgers, why not make tacos instead? It's all the same stuff, except you need to add a packet of taco seasoning and use soft flour tortillas, which take up less room than hamburger rolls. Such simple variations offer endless possibilities.

CHAPTER THREE

Cooking Tips

GRILLING: HOW TO AVOID FLAMING DISASTERS

The Proper Fire

First, forget about starting the fire with any sort of liquid charcoal lighter. Lighter fluid is popular because it appears to do the job dramatically and quickly. A douse of fluid, a lighted match, and it's a wonderful sound and light show, just like an alchemist from the Middle Ages magically creating gold.

Other methods for lighting charcoal are not only more efficient; they also do not leave a residue that can be tasted in the food, as some lighter fluid does. It's far better to arrange the charcoal into a cone shape and use a fire-starting brick to get things going.

Then it's all a matter of patience—the willingness to wait until the fire is at the proper stage before starting to grill. That's the secret to good grilling. Charcoal needs between 30 and 45 minutes before the coals are ready, where the briquets have both a white coating and a fiery ring around them. Then, and only then, should you start cooking.

A grilling fire should always be under control. Flames should never touch the food. If you try to cook with a wild fire where the flames come in contact with the meat, the outside of the food will end up scorched while the inside remains raw. Yuck.

Sticky Grills

Even when a grate is clean, food will sometimes stick to it, making it impossible to flip burgers or turn chicken breasts without tearing them apart. The best remedy: a quick shot of vegetable spray before you place the grating over the fire. The spray will act like a temporary Teflon and make the food far easier to manipulate. Vegetable sprays normally do not contain salt, so they will not cause the grating or other parts of the grill to rust. If anything, vegetable sprays actually help prolong the life of a grill's grate.

Wait at least five minutes for the rack to warm up. That not only provides a better cooking surface, it also kills any bacteria that might be on the grating.

Marinades

A number of recipes in this book call for soaking meat in marinades before grilling. Marinades furnish an array of flavors that are impossible to obtain any other way, even with gravies, by allowing additional flavors to seep into the food.

Meat should marinate for at least 30 to 60 minutes, longer if it can be refrigerated. Vegetables, which are apt to turn mushy if marinated too long, usually need less than 30 minutes. Always use a nonaluminum container for holding marinades. Glass bowls work well, but resealable plastic bags are even better.

Beware of Charring

Many marinades and barbecue sauces have a lot of sugar, which chars easily over an open flame and forms an unappetizing crusty, sootlike layer on the outside. For this reason, whenever cooking ribs or chicken, try parboiling first to reduce the grilling time. Or employ indirect heat, with the meat on one side of the grill and the heat on the other. Good indirect heat is also obtained either by putting all the charcoal in the middle of the grill and cooking at the edges or by using aluminum foil. If you have a gas grill, grill sugary items on the second rack.

Avoid Excessive Flip Flopping

Although it may be tempting because you often see it done in the movies, *do not* turn the food the first few minutes it is on the grill. That's when the coating forms that seals in the juices.

Avoid Sharp Objects

Use tongs or a spatula—never a fork—to turn food on the grill. A fork allows the juices, which are supposed to remain sealed in and which add so much of the flavor, to escape.

Hold the Salt

Many grill cooks recommend not putting salt on meat before or during grilling. The reason: The salt will tend to dry the food out. I've had mixed results with this approach, but it does make sense in theory. On the other hand, soy sauce, a popular grilling marinade, is loaded with salt.

Cooking Items of Varying Thickness

The easiest approach is to start cooking the thickest item first, since it will take the longest. Another method is to bank or stack more coals to one side of the grill so that one side will be hotter. This not only allows you simultaneously to cook foods of varying size, it also is a good way to keep some items warm while cooking others.

Cooking Thoroughly

Hygiene is especially important for outdoor cooks when it comes to fresh meat. Meat should be refrigerated as long as possible and should still be cool (but not the slightest bit frozen) when it first touches the grill. That will help to control and kill any bacteria.

Do not reuse containers or plates that have fresh meat juices on them without washing them first.

Hamburgers should be cooked thoroughly: Any bacteria that was on the surface of the meat when it was ground gets distributed throughout the hamburger.

COOKING WITH ALUMINUM FOIL

Cooking with aluminum foil when grilling or cooking over an open fire seems to be a lost art, perhaps because of our concern about the environment and the greater emphasis on recycling. Some people also appear wary of aluminum foil and aluminum pans because of the possible link between aluminum and Alzheimer's disease.

Experts say, however, that if you really want to reduce the amount of aluminum that enters your system, don't worry about aluminum cookware or the aluminum in deodorants. Instead, be careful about how much aluminum you ingest from pickled foods: The alum is a double sulfate of aluminum and potassium.

Only a few recipes in this book specifically talk about using aluminum foil, but many other recipes certainly could be adapted to this technique. The advantage of cooking with aluminum foil is that it's possible to divide up foods that have different cooking times and start them accordingly. Aluminum foil also cooks foods fairly quickly and prevents the juices/moisture from escaping. Furthermore, once the food is served, the cooking foil can do double duty as serving platters or plates.

Cooking Methods

Thick, heavy-duty aluminum foil is best for outdoor cooking, because the thinner type is apt to puncture more easily. However, you can always make a double or triple liner out of the thin stuff if that's all you have. When you use foil in cooking, the duller side of the foil (if there is a duller side) should be on the outside. And the foil should be tightly sealed so that none of the juices escape.

There are several good ways to seal foil so the juices don't drip out. For apples, potatoes, corn, and the like, roll the items up in the foil and twist each end, like candy wrappers. This also makes it easy to turn them so they cook thoroughly on all sides. When cooking several items together, such as meat and vegetables, arrange the items in a square shape on one side of the foil, then fold the piece of foil over so that only three sides—not four—have to be folded and sealed. Each of the three edges should be folded at least two or three times to ensure against leaks. Folding the foil on the sides instead of on the top allows the food to cook more evenly when it is turned over.

Meats can be tightly sealed, with very little, if any, excess space. The flavor of vegetables, on the other hand, can be enhanced by wrapping them more loosely, which allows the steam inside to mix the flavors more fully.

Cooking Times for Foil

With a wood fire, use a stick to flatten part of the fire and then place some ash over the coals before cooking the foil packet. You can speed up the cooking time by placing coals or hot ash on top of the package, which will then cook on both sides, eliminating the need for turning.

Because every wood fire is different, you may need to experiment to learn the proper cooking times, but here are some good general guidelines. An item that is about two inches thick probably needs about 20 minutes— 10 minutes on each side. A large item like a chicken may require as much as an hour.

Whole potatoes and onions may also require an hour to cook fully, so place them at the edge of the fire and turn regularly. Vegetables cooked beside an open fire rather than in it can be placed in position as soon as the fire is started. Don't wait until there are good cooking coals, which may not occur until after the first hour. Quartering and dicing vegetables will speed up their cooking time dramatically.

Once a foil packet is removed from the fire, it soon cools to the temperature of the food it contains—but it may still be so hot that you want to wear a pair of cotton gloves to open the packet.

BAKING OUTDOORS

Baking outdoors has always been a challenge, and until recently, there has been no good method for doing this when you're packing light. In a pinch, two aluminum pie pans sealed together with metal clips would bake bread, brownies, and cakes, but that was about all this makeshift outfit was good for. Fortunately, advances in equipment have made baking a much surer way to cook. But first, let's look at some of the older methods.

The Dutch Oven

The Dutch oven is still a very reliable way to bake if you are able to tote along one of these heavy cooking pots. Dutch ovens come in various sizes. Unless you are planning to feed an army, an eight-inch Dutch oven will hold enough to provide the main course for three to five people. A Dutch oven, usually made of cast iron, can be placed directly over the flame. Many of the ovens have three legs to set them above the fire; those that don't can be lifted off the ground with a couple of stones or rocks. What makes the Dutch oven so effective is the cover, which has a raised lip that permits hot coals or lighted briquets to be placed on top of the container. Heating the oven from both above and below is what turns an otherwise ordinary cooking pot into a true oven.

A cast-iron Dutch oven cooks more evenly than any aluminum container, but cast iron does require considerable care. A new Dutch oven has to be seasoned so food won't stick to it. Some people claim the best way to season a new oven (as well as a cast-iron skillet) is to cook three or four pounds of bacon in it, then liberally douse the insides with bacon fat. Next, bake the empty pot in a conventional oven for an hour or so.

To clean a Dutch oven (or any cast-iron pan), simply wipe it down with a paper towel to remove anything sticking to the bottom or side, then use a fresh paper towel to re-oil the inside. Plain water is fine for removing encrusted debris, but never use soap for cleaning, since soap destroys the seasoning.

Lightweight Ovens

The Coleman company has made some wonderful items, but their folding, collapsible oven never has been one of them. Such ovens just aren't airtight enough to bake quickly. However, once such an oven is set up at the campsite, you can improve its performance by wrapping the top and sides with aluminum foil. But you need to leave the temperature gauge visible and also make it possible to fold back the foil so you can open the door and check on the contents. Although this oven is easily transportable, it's still too heavy for most backpackers.

So let's all praise the inventors of the lightweight but very efficient Outback Oven, which is a brilliant improvement over the old aluminum pie-pan technique mentioned above. The Outback Oven, a true oven that will bake pizzas, breads, pies, and casseroles, comes in several sizes, including one that is only seven ounces, an ideal weight for backpackers.

Basically, the Outback Oven is a convection oven that consists of two round pans that fit together like a casserole dish, except that the pans separate in the middle. When used on a stove, the oven employs a stainless steel diffuser plate placed on top of the burner to better disperse the heat, plus a circular riser bar that holds the oven above the diffuser plate.

An aluminized fiberglass fabric goes over the cooking pans to hold and reflect back the heat while also directing it upward. This system works so efficiently that you can cook items like rice, cakes, and pies about as quickly at camp as you can at home.

The Outback Oven comes in several sizes, but the largest, the Outback Oven Plus 10, is the most versatile. At 24 ounces, the outfit is the perfect size for many store-bought mixes, such as brownies and cakes. The smaller ovens require you to cut the mixes, which can sometimes be a problem. Makers of the Outback Oven also offer a variety of mixes (pizzas, paella, lasagna) that only need water added. For more information, contact Traveling Light, 1563 Solano Ave., Suite 284, Berkeley, CA 94707, (800) 299-0378, fax (510) 526-8701.

CHAPTER FOUR

All-Around Sauces

In many recipes calling for butter, olive oil can be substituted for butter or margarine so that backpackers can carry them without fear of spoiling.

Jerk It!
No, this is not about the old Steve Martin movie of the same name. Jerk is the Jamaican name for outdoor grilling, which traditionally has been done in 55-gallon drums split lengthwise and turned into grills. Despite the odd name, jerk seasoning is among the best in the world—very spicy, very flavorful, sometimes very hot, but always incredibly delicious.

No one really knows how jerk got its name. Some say it's because the meat is "jerked" on the grill by being turned over and over again. Others say it's because the meat is jerked off the bone with a fork when it is served.

It really doesn't matter. What is important is that jerk goes on anything: beef, poultry, fish, lamb, whatever. It can also be used to spice up a lot of vegetable dishes, such as rice and squash. The only thing I haven't tried jerk on is eggs.

Commercially prepared jerk seasonings are becoming more available in regular grocery stores as more people become familiar with jerk. Buy them, try them, and use them on some of the recipes in the grilling section. Or make it from scratch ahead of time, put it in a glass jar, and carry it with you on camping trips.

Once you taste jerk, it will become a regular part of your diet. The last time I was in Jamaica, I brought home 18 jars of the three different varieties. When I run out, I'll be back to using the following recipes.

DRY JERK SEASONING

This is not as hot as the others, and this is the type of seasoning McCormick has recently started selling. It doesn't require any exotic spices, so this is a good first introduction to jerk. If you like it, get more adventurous and try the others. Excellent for meats and especially vegetables. To increase the temperature, add more cayenne pepper. This makes only about 5 tablespoons, so there's little left over.

1 tsp allspice
1 tsp cayenne pepper
1 Tbl onion flakes
1 Tbl onion powder
2 tsp thyme
2 tsp salt
1/4 tsp ground nutmeg
1/4 tsp ground cinnamon
1 tsp black pepper
2 tsp sugar

Simply blend it all together and store in a glass container.

JERK PASTE

This is used to rub over the meat before grilling. Use a blender or food processor to mix it thoroughly. This makes a cup, more than you'll need for any one occasion, so put leftovers in the refrigerator for later use. This is not only spicy; it can be quite hot, depending on the peppers used. The hottest are the habanero and Scotch bonnet. Milder are the readily available jalapeno or serrano peppers. You know how much heat you can stand.

2 tsp thyme leaves
1 tsp ground allspice
1/4 tsp ground nutmeg
1/2 tsp ground cinnamon
4–6 hot peppers, finely ground
2 tsp salt
1 medium onion, finely chopped
1/2 cup finely chopped scallions
1 tsp black pepper

Mix everything together in a blender to create a paste. Then store in a glass jar in a refrigerator.

JERK MARINADE

Also called wet jerk seasoning, this is my favorite type of jerk. I use it constantly to grill chicken, and I never get tired of it. You can turn up the heat by adding more peppers. This makes about 1 1/2 cups and can be stored in the refrigerator.

1 Tbl olive oil
2 Tbl cider vinegar
1 tsp black pepper
1 onion, finely chopped
1/2 cup scallion, finely chopped
2 tsp thyme
2 tsp allspice
1 tsp salt
2 tsp sugar
1 hot pepper
1/2 tsp ground nutmeg
1/2 tsp ground cinnamon

Simply mix everything together. A food processor works better than a blender because it leaves tiny chunks of pepper and onion.

BASIL BUTTER

This wonderful blend can be used on steamed veggies or on grilled meats, including fish. This can be prepared ahead of time and kept frozen indefinitely.

2 small onions
8 Tbl butter or olive oil
1 tsp Dijon mustard
1/2 tsp lemon juice
1/2 cup sweet basil leaves

1. Mince onions. Soften butter in a warm pan. Add onions, basil, mustard, and lemon juice. Simmer until onions are soft.

2. Refrigerate until needed. Freeze in a long roll and slice off as needed.

CREAMY SALAD DRESSING FOR ANYTHING

A basic, all-around dressing for any sort of mixed greens.

1 tsp minced garlic
1 tsp basil leaves
3 Tbl olive oil
1 Tbl red wine vinegar
1 Tbl chopped chives
1 Tbl oregano leaves
2 Tbl plain nonfat yogurt or milk

1. Mix all ingredients in container with lid. Shake vigorously.

2. Spoon over salad.

BASIL PESTO

This needs to be mixed thoroughly in a blender or food processor, so prepare it before leaving home. Store in a small jar.

2 Tbl minced garlic
3 cups sweet basil leaves
1/2 tsp olive oil
1/4 cup chopped walnuts (pine nuts would be even better)
1/4 cup Parmesan cheese

1. Puree garlic, basil, and olive oil.

2. Add nuts and cheese and blend until nuts are BB-sized.

3. Store. This should be served over hot cooked vermicelli or linguine. For added flavor, warm the pesto sauce before pouring it over noodles.

EASY ONION GRAVY

Goes well with mashed potatoes, on meats, whatever—and it couldn't be simpler to make.

1 package dry onion soup mix
1 small onion, sliced (optional)
1 tsp minced garlic
3 Tbl butter, margarine, or olive oil

1. Prepare dry soup mix according to directions. If you want more onion, saute the small sliced onion and garlic in butter until the onion is soft.

2. Add sauteed onion and garlic to soup mix. Let simmer for 3–5 minutes.

MANGO CHUTNEY

This is a wonderful accompaniment to curries and other spicy dishes. Chutney is quite expensive in the stores, and after you see the ingredients in this recipe, you'll see why. The following makes a huge quantity that can be prepared at home and refrigerated.

6 green, unripe mangoes (should be hard)
5 cups vinegar
3/4 cup brown sugar
2 tsp chopped fresh mint
2 tsp ground ginger
8 green chilies, chopped
1 1/2 tsp salt
3 large bananas
1 cup seedless raisins

Garnish
1/2 tsp cumin
1 1/2 tsp coriander
6 cardamom seeds
18 whole cloves
2 bay leaves

1. In a large pan, mix together all the ingredients except garnish and boil for 5–10 minutes, until fruit is tender.

2. Put the garnish in a muslin bag and add to the fruit pan. Continue cooking until the mix begins to thicken.

3. Remove the muslin bag and discard. Allow the chutney to cool, or refrigerate, before serving.

BEARNAISE SAUCE

This easy sauce goes well with egg dishes, meats, and vegetables. It's available for purchase in instant packets, but it's very easy to make.

3 Tbl wine vinegar
2 tsp parsley
2 tsp dried tarragon
2 egg yolks
8 Tbl butter (4 oz)
1 Tbl chopped onion

1. Boil the vinegar with the herbs until it is reduced to only about 3 tsp. Strain into a bowl and stir in the egg yolks. Warm butter.

2. Place the bowl over simmering hot water and stir until the eggs begin to cook. Do not allow eggs to harden; stir them constantly, and even remove the bowl from the hot water if they begin to harden.

3. Continuing to stir the eggs, add the melted butter spoon by spoon. Mixture should become thick, like a cream.

MOCK HOLLANDAISE SAUCE

Real hollandaise sauce is almost pure butter. In the interest of clear arteries, this substitutes quite well for serving over steak, eggs, fish, or vegetables—especially asparagus.

1 10 1/2-oz can cream of mushroom soup
1 Tbl lemon juice
1/4 cup mayonnaise (low-fat or fat-free)

Combine everything and cook over low heat until the mixture begins to thicken. Serve warm.

CREOLE SAUCE

A quick and easy sauce for eggs and meats. This makes about 2 cups.

1 small green pepper, cubed
1 small onion, sliced
2 Tbl butter, margarine, or olive oil
1 10 1/2-oz can condensed tomato soup
1/4 cup water
1 tsp vinegar
Hot sauce to taste

1. Saute the onion and green pepper in butter or margarine until tender.

2. Add other ingredients and cook uncovered for 5 minutes over low heat.

CHAPTER FIVE

Breakfast Ideas

The typical breakfast is usually uninspired, something slapped together while everyone is packing up, or—worse—the same old stuff. Chipped beef on toast didn't become known as "SOS" for nothing.

These fresh ideas will definitely enliven the break of day. Eggs are a staple part of many of these recipes, but there are also some items, such as chili, that traditionally would be associated with lunch or dinner. But if you're going to be putting in a long, active day, you need a hearty meal at breakfast, not at dinner, when you're often too tired to enjoy fixing or eating anything.

SPICY LEFTOVER STEAK

How often have you cooked steak and discovered that you were more than generous in your estimates and there are lots of leftovers? This can happen easily with something like a London broil, which is a big piece of meat, anyway.

Warmed-up steak tastes better than reheated chicken, but that's not saying much. This is the most flavorful way I know to make leftover steak as good as—if not better than—when it was first cooked!

1. Slice leftover steak into strips and let it warm to the natural temperature. If it's cold, make adjustments accordingly and somehow try to get the steak in the 60–70 degree range but *do not* reheat over a stove! This recipe makes about 1 1/2 cups of sauce.

1 package Knorr pepper sauce mix
1/4 cup white wine
1 Tbl chopped onion
3 Tbl plain yogurt
1 1/2 cups water

2. In skillet, mix water and Knorr sauce and bring to boil. Stir constantly. Then reduce heat and simmer for 2 minutes, stirring frequently.

3. Take the skillet off the fire and remove peppercorns with slotted spoon or strainer and discard. Remove sauce from skillet and place in bowl.

4. Add onion and white wine to skillet and cook over low heat until reduced by half. Stir in peppercorn sauce and add yogurt.

5. Simmer for 5 minutes, then pour over steak. Yes, this would even improve a fresh cut of meat of dubious quality.

HAM AND PINEAPPLE CURRY

Even people who think they don't like curry will love this dish. Serves 4.

2 cups cooked ham
8-oz can pineapple chunks and juice
1 cup chicken bouillon
1 medium onion, chopped
1 tsp minced garlic
1/2 tsp ground ginger
2 Tbl margarine
2 Tbl curry powder
2 Tbl all-purpose flour
2 carrots, sliced
1 Tbl catsup
4–6 cups cooked rice

1. In a skillet, cook garlic and onion in margarine until onion is tender. Add curry powder and ginger and cook 1 more minute. Stir in flour.

2. Drain pineapple, pouring juice into skillet. Place pineapple aside. Add catsup, carrots, and chicken bouillon. Bring to boil, then reduce to simmer, cover, and cook for 15 minutes.

3. Stir in ham and pineapple chunks. Heat both thoroughly. Serve over hot rice.

THE PERFECT OMELETTE

And it only takes 40 seconds to cook. Water is used instead of milk to make the eggs fluffier, and margarine is used because it's less likely to burn than butter. The key is to concentrate on cooking the eggs and not the filling, since the filling will cook much slower. Cook or warm the filling mixture and have it ready to add. This is an omelette for 1.

2 eggs (or powdered eggs)
1/2 tsp salt
2 Tbl water
1 Tbl margarine
1/2 cup your favorite diced meats or veggies, already cooked
Black pepper to taste
Hot sauce (optional)

1. In a bowl, beat together eggs, salt, and water. Heat margarine in skillet until it sizzles when a drop of water is added.

2. Pour in egg mixture. Use a spatula and tilt the skillet to move the egg mixture around so that it cooks evenly.

3. Once the egg mixture no longer flows, pour the 1/2 cup of chopped ham, green peppers, whatever, on half of the egg. With the spatula, fold over the other half of the omelette. Slide onto serving plate. Use pepper and hot sauce to taste.

BANANA RUM OMELETTE, FLAMBÉ

Now to the spicy variety, with the always-wonderful Caribbean flair. Flambe is not something most people consume at a camp breakfast, so this will definitely make an impression. For 2.

4 eggs or powdered eggs
3 Tbl water
3 Tbl margarine
1/4 tsp salt
1/4 tsp pepper
3 Tbl rum or rum extract

Filling
2 small bananas or 1 large one
2 Tbl margarine
1 tsp nutmeg
1 tsp cinnamon
1 Tbl honey (optional)

1. Since the filling will take longer, prepare it first. Slice the banana and saute in margarine with nutmeg and cinnamon (and honey, if desired). Set aside.

2. Heat skillet with margarine until it sizzles when a drop of water is added. In the meantime, beat eggs together with the water, salt, and pepper and begin to cook. Once the eggs no longer run, add filling to onehalf of the omelette and, with a spatula, fold over the other half and serve on a plate.

3. Pour on the rum and set afire. When flame is almost out, cut in half and serve.

JAMAICAN RUM TOAST

Forget French toast, a boring and tasteless cousin of this far more flavorful version. I first had this at the Half Moon Club in Montego Bay. It's exceptional. A simpler variation is to use cinnamon sugar in place of all the flavorings except the rum. As for syrup, forget it—this recipe packs its own, in the batter. For 2–4.

1 cup milk
4 eggs
4 Tbl sugar
2 oz rum (or rum extract)
1 Tbl nutmeg
1 Tbl allspice
1/2 tsp vanilla
3 Tbl margarine
4–6 thick slices of bread (especially raisin bread)

1. Mix all the ingredients except margarine in a bowl and keep them warm so they don't separate. Heat margarine in skillet until it sizzles when a drop of water is added.

2. Drape bread through batter mix. Add to skillet and cook until golden brown on each side. If the bread is a little soft (but not soggy) in the middle, so much the better.

BASIL POTATOES

These can be served with the above omelette or with any main course. Potatoes often seem like a lot of trouble to cook in the morning, so boil them the night before while you're eating dinner. Serves 3–4.

4 potatoes, sliced
1 small onion, sliced
3 Tbl olive oil
3 Tbl basil leaves
1 Tbl garlic salt
Black pepper to taste
Hot sauce to taste (optional)

Heat the oil in a skillet and add the onions. Cook onions for about 3 minutes. Coat the sliced potatoes with basil and garlic salt and black pepper. Fry for about 5 minutes. Let folks add their own hot sauce.

FLANK STEAK DIABLO

When you want a hearty breakfast, this steak served with eggs will get you going and energize you throughout the day. This is absolutely delicious for breakfast. Serves 4.

1 medium flank steak
Meat tenderizer
Tabasco Sauce
Black pepper

1. Rub meat tenderizer into flank steak and let stand for 15 minutes. Then rub Tabasco Sauce and black pepper into the meat.

2. Grill or pan fry on medium-high for 3–4 minutes on each side. Add a few drops of Tabasco to both sides when the steak is done.

3. Since flank steak can be a tough piece of meat, how you cut it for serving is essential. Carve it diagonally into french-fry-sized slices; hold your knife at about 45 degrees when you're cutting.

VEGETARIAN CHILI

Meat is just another ingredient in many stews and soups, a broad range that would also include chili. No one's likely to notice that it isn't even there. But if you must have your meat, simply brown a pound of lean hamburger or ground turkey and add it to the pot. This can be made ahead of time and part of it carried by backpackers, since 4 pounds of cans is an awful lot to add to someone's pack. This recipe, good for breakfast, lunch, or dinner, serves 4–6.

2 1-lb cans of tomato sauce
2 1-lb cans of kidney beans (or hot chili beans)
1 bell pepper, cut into strips
1 onion, chopped
1 1-lb can of tomatoes (whole or otherwise)
2 Tbl chili powder
1 Tbl garlic salt
1 Tbl basil leaves
Hot sauce to taste

1. Mix all ingredients in a skillet. Bring to a simmer, cover, and cook for at least 30 minutes. The longer this cooks, the better the flavors will blend, but the beans will also get mushier. If you cook this over low heat for an hour or two, don't add the beans until the last 30 minutes. Stir regularly, regardless of cooking time.

2. Serve with grated cheese on top, with crackers or bread, and/or with your favorite hot sauce.

BERRIES-N-CREAM

This could actually be a dessert served anytime, but it's also a good way to keep stomachs satisfied until breakfast is ready. Serves 4.

1 quart nonfat yogurt or sour cream
1 pint fresh blueberries or strawberries
2 tsp ground nutmeg
Maple syrup

1. Sweeten berries with a light coating of maple syrup. Mix well with yogurt or sour cream.

2. Scoop berries-n-cream into 4 bowls. Top each one with half a tsp of the ground nutmeg. Taste and add more if desired. A little nutmeg can go a long way.

HUEVOS RANCHEROS

A classic, spicy egg dish that is a great way to meet the day. Serves 2 hungry campers.

4 eggs
1 cup medium or hot picante sauce
1 tsp minced garlic
2 Tbl olive oil
4 tortillas
1 1/2 tsp minced onion (optional)
1/2 tsp marjoram
1 16-oz can refried beans

1. Saute onion, garlic, marjoram, and picante sauce in olive oil to combine flavors.

2. Either poach the eggs on top of sauce or fry eggs separately.

3. Place eggs and sauce over warm tortillas. Serve with heated refried beans.

EGGS, CHEESE, AND HAM OLÉ

A spicy version of another Mexican breakfast. Using 2 eggs per person, this serves 4.

8 eggs
4 Tbl butter
8 slices of cheddar cheese
1 cup diced ham
1/2 cup medium or hot picante sauce
4 tsp sliced olives
1/4 cup sweet pickle relish
Salt and pepper to taste (optional)

1. In the following order, place cheese, ham, and relish in buttered baking dish.

2. Place uncooked eggs on top of this sauce. Then add a tsp of picante sauce over the top of each egg. Bake at 300°F (160°C).

3. Once the egg whites are firm, and while the yolk is still soft but not runny, remove container from oven. Allow everyone to serve themselves and add sliced olives, salt, and pepper.

PEPPERONI EGG PIZZA

This is certainly not a traditional Italian dish. If you want to make this a complete and very filling breakfast and more pizzalike, serve the eggs over hamburger buns or wrap them in warm tortillas. This serves 4.

8 eggs (real or powdered)
4 oz sliced pepperoni
1/2 green bell pepper, cubed
1 small onion, sliced
2 Tbl olive oil
2 Tbl sliced olives
Parmesan cheese
1 cup pizza sauce (optional—try it both ways)

1. Saute onion and green pepper in olive oil. Drain excess liquid, add pepperoni, and cook for about 2 minutes.

2. In a bowl, scramble the eggs and add to skillet. Also add sliced olives. Cook eggs and stir constantly so pepper, pepperoni, olives, and onion become well mixed.

3. Once the eggs are cooked, let people help themselves and add their own pizza sauce and Parmesan cheese.

EGGS BENEDICT
(with Smoked Turkey)

Another classic breakfast, ideal for special occasions. Try this with deli-smoked turkey breast for something really different. Serves 4.

4 hamburger rolls or English muffins
8 slices Canadian bacon, ham, or smoked turkey
1 package Knorr hollandaise sauce or mock hollandaise sauce
8 poached eggs
Margarine for cooking

1. To poach eggs, place 2 inches of water in pan and bring to a boil. Then reduce to a simmer. Break eggs on a plate and slide into the water. Cook for 3–5 minutes. You'll need a slotted spatula to divide and remove the eggs.

2. While eggs are cooking, prepare hollandaise sauce according to directions. Once eggs are cooked, place them in a warm container and discard water. Heat meat and buttered, halved rolls together in a skillet.

3. On each roll half, place a slice of meat and an egg, then liberally ladle hollandaise sauce over each egg.

HAM ROLLS

As good as these are, don't get carried away or they could become your full meal. On second thought, that's not so bad. Serves 4–6.

1/8 cup olive oil
2 Tbl prepared mustard
1 tsp oregano
1 small onion, finely chopped
1 tsp Worcestershire sauce
1/2 lb thinly sliced ham
1/2 lb Swiss cheese
4 hot dog rolls

1. Slice each hot dog roll into two rolls.

2. Mix together oil, mustard, oregano, onion, and Worcestershire sauce and spread on hot dog rolls.

3. Place ham and cheese on rolls. Bake at 350°F (180°C) for 10 minutes.

CHAPTER SIX

Veggies and Vegetarian Dishes

Being Irish, I was raised on potatoes like they were mother's milk. But not all potatoes are created equal, and some are far better for certain styles of cooking than others. For my money, the best are the round, red-skinned spuds, sometimes called "new potatoes." The moisture content —and natural taste—of these are far better than that of the large brown-skinned potatoes, the Russets, the Idaho, and the long white all-purpose types.

The best way to illustrate this is to steam a red-skinned potato and a Russet or Idaho in a colander. Once they're done, cut the potatoes open and take a taste. The red-skinneds are moist and flavorful; they can be eaten just as they are. The Russets and Idahos, however, will be dry and mealy and require great doses of butter, sour cream, and bacon bits to make them palatable, or they will need to be mashed with milk.

In all of the recipes calling for potatoes, use the red-skinned kind unless you are fortunate enough to find easy access to a scarcer variety called Yukon Gold, which has a natural creamy texture and buttery flavor.

Check chapter 5 for the wonderful Basil Potatoes.

As you'll note, there are quite a few potato recipes in this chapter. There are two reasons for that. First, potatoes are easy to pack and take almost anywhere, and they don't need to be refrigerated. Second, with the skins left on, they are a well-balanced food. It's the toppings that make potatoes so fattening, not the potato itself.

Improving Canned Vegetables
These can be improved dramatically by this simple technique: Whatever the vegetable, drain the liquid into a cooking pan and boil it until it is reduced by half. Lower the heat and add the vegetables and other seasonings and cook quickly but do not boil.

POTATOES IN FOIL

Figure on 1/4 to 1/2 pound of potatoes per person. This recipe is for 2 hungry campers.

1 lb small red-skinned potatoes
1 yellow onion
1/2 cup olive oil or butter
1/4 tsp nutmeg (optional)
Salt and pepper to taste

1. Wash potatoes, cut into halves, and place in bowl with olive oil (and optional nutmeg). Stir quickly and place potatoes on a sheet of heavy-duty aluminum foil. The oil will help keep the potatoes from sticking to the foil as they cook.

2. Slice the onion thinly and place a slice atop each potato half. Sprinkle with salt and pepper. Seal the foil to form a bag.

3. Place on heated grill or in campfire after gray ash has formed on coals. Bake for 30 minutes and test. A fork should easily penetrate to the middle of a potato, but don't let the potato become too soft or mushy.

SPICY ROASTED POTATOES

Use the smallest red-skinned ("new") potatoes possible. Figure on 4–6 per person, depending on their size. These can be prepared in a container over a fire or in an oven. The results are guaranteed delicious regardless of how you prepare them.

Red potatoes with their skins
1 Tbl minced garlic
1 Tbl basil leaves
1 Tbl oregano leaves
1/4 cup olive oil

1. Mix everything but the potatoes in cooking container. Add potatoes and coat them well.

2. Begin cooking in an uncovered container over medium heat. Check occasionally and roll the potatoes in the mixture. Depending on the size

of the potatoes, they could be done in just 15–20 minutes. To make the skin crisper, drain all the liquid and cook for another 3–5 minutes, turning once.

SMASHED TATERS WITH NUTMEG

The first time I had mashed potatoes with nutmeg, I couldn't believe the taste. I'd always thought mashed potatoes needed gravy to taste really good. What this does to instant potatoes, which generally need all the help they can get, is incredible. Serves 6. Leftovers can be used to make potato pancakes at breakfast.

8 large red potatoes or 8 medium white potatoes
2 Tbl garlic salt
1/2 cup nonfat sour cream (or milk)
1/2 tsp nutmeg
6 Tbl butter or margarine

1. Leaving on the skin (which has most of the vitamins), boil potatoes in water containing the garlic salt.

2. Drain potatoes and mash with butter.

3. Add sour cream and nutmeg and mash again. You may want to add more nutmeg, perhaps pepper. There will be a hint of garlic already.

HOT-N-SPICY POTATO PANCAKES

Those leftover smashed taters that were being referred to a second ago? This is how to prepare them.

Optional additions
1 small onion, diced
Tabasco Sauce

1. Form potatoes into flat patties. Saute in your choice of butter, margarine, or olive oil.

2. Turn at least once, cooking until potatoes are golden brown. Let folks add their own hot sauce.

GRILLED ONIONS

I could eat cooked onions with every meal. These will cook best if you have a ceramic accessory that you can place directly atop the grill in order to keep small, delicate foods from dropping into the fire. Or if you're using an open fire, use a hamburger cradle. The following is for 6 people; leftovers can always be heated up and added to burgers or whatever.

1/2 cup olive oil
6 red onions (or fresh, sweet Vidalias from Georgia if you can find them)
1/4 cup apple cider vinegar
1/2 tsp garlic salt

1. Mix oil, vinegar, and garlic salt together in a bowl or jar.

2. Peel and slice the onions in half, horizontally. Add onions to vinegar and oil and marinate for 2 hours. It is not necessary to chill them.

3. Cook onions on grill for about 10 minutes per side. Baste occasionally to keep them from drying out.

ROASTED GARLIC

Simple, delicious, and another favorite. This recipe is for 4, but it is easy to increase or decrease. Plan to serve one entire head of garlic per person. Leftovers can be added to other meals.

4 garlic heads
8 Tbl olive oil
Black pepper

1. Peel skin off each head of garlic. Open the head without breaking off any of the individual cloves. Sprinkle each head with 2 drops of oil and a dash of black pepper.

2. Wrap each garlic head individually in heavy-duty aluminum foil. Heat atop grill or beside open fire for about 30 minutes, turning the packets about every 5 minutes. Cook until the head is soft.

CURRIED CORN

Corn and beans have all the essential proteins needed for survival. You never knew canned corn could taste so good. This serves 2–3, but the recipe can easily be doubled by adding a second can of corn.

1/8 cup butter, margarine, or olive oil
1 17-oz can of corn, drained
2 Tbl chopped green sweet bell pepper
2 Tbl chopped red pepper or pimiento
(or, in place of the peppers, use 1/2 cup of chopped radishes)
2 Tbl chopped onion
1 tsp curry powder
1/2 cup sour cream

1. In a skillet, melt the butter, then add curry powder and all the other ingredients, except the sour cream. Cook for 8–10 minutes over low heat.

2. Stir in the sour cream. Stir constantly until the mixture is thoroughly heated.

BBQ CORN

Nothing is easier to transport and cook than fresh ears of corn. And if it's fresh out of the field, nothing is sweeter. But even a good ear of corn can be spiced up.

4 ears of corn, unhusked
1/4 cup butter or margarine (or olive oil)
1 Tbl prepared BBQ sauce

1. To grill, leave the husks on the corn but remove the silk. Let soak in water for at least an hour. Then place corn on grill grate and cook for 30 minutes.

2. To boil the corn, remove the husk and all the silk. In a covered pot of boiling water, cook the corn for 3–5 minutes.

3. While the corn is cooking, soften butter and mix it with your favorite barbecue sauce.

SAUCY CORN

This is another good flavoring for fresh corn if you think the BBQ sauce might detract too much from the corn's natural flavor.

1/4 cup butter or margarine
1/2 tsp oregano
1/4 tsp garlic salt

Soften the butter/margarine and mix all ingredients together thoroughly.

HORSERADISH BEETS

Beets are one of our most underused vegetables, perhaps because beets can be blah without the right seasonings. This recipe, which serves 2–4, goes especially well with either pork or beef. Taste the sauce before serving; you might want more horseradish.

1 16-oz can or 2 cups of fresh beets
2 Tbl flour
1 cup milk
3 Tbl horseradish
2 Tbl margarine
Salt to taste

1. Cook beets (boil) if necessary. Chop them into small cubes and keep them warm.

2. In a skillet, melt the margarine, then stir in the flour. Add milk slowly, stirring continually, until the mixture becomes smooth. Add the horseradish and mix thoroughly.

3. Pour over warm beets, add salt to taste, and serve immediately.

QUICK BBQ BEANS

This is a fast way to spice up canned baked beans so that everyone will be wanting more. Serves 4.

2 16-oz cans baked beans
2 Tbl prepared mustard
1 medium onion, chopped
1/2 bell pepper, chopped
1 cup your favorite BBQ sauce

1. Drain beans of all liquid and place in a skillet. Add chopped onion, green pepper, mustard, and BBQ sauce.

2. Cook over medium-low heat for about 5 minutes, until pepper and onion are soft. Taste to see if you want more BBQ sauce.

SPICY VEGETABLES COOKED IN FOIL

Lots of variations of this recipe are possible according to the season and your favorite veggies. The following are in season almost all the time. Serves 3–4.

6 carrots
6 small onions
3 celery sticks
1 medium green pepper
One of the sauces listed below

1. Peel carrots and onion. Slice pepper in half and remove the seeds. Leave onions whole but cut carrots and celery into quarters and green pepper into strips.

2. Divide the vegetables into individual packets, 3 or 4, depending on the number to be fed.

3. If you want only the taste of vegetables, add black pepper and garlic salt to taste.

4. Or add 1 Tbl of BBQ sauce to each packet.

5. Or 1 Tbl Italian salad dressing per packet.

6. Or 1/2 tsp dry jerk seasoning per packet.

7. Or 3–5 drops hot sauce per packet.

8. Cook at edge of fire for about 20 minutes.

FRESH TOMATOES OREGANO

This assumes, of course, that you have some way to get the tomatoes to camp without mushing them. A hard, plastic container works well. Allow 1/2 tomato per person. Good with almost anything. Serves 2.

1 whole tomato
2 tsp olive oil
1 tsp oregano leaves
Salt and pepper to taste
2–4 drops hot sauce (optional)

1. Cut tomatoes in half. Mix all the ingredients and baste the cut side of each tomato with them.

2. Place each tomato in its own piece of foil. Place on grill, cut side down, for 3–5 minutes. This also works well broiled in an oven, without the foil.

SPICED SWEET POTATOES AND APPLES

For some reason, a lot of cooks like to add sugar to foods that are already naturally sweet. The only reason I can find to account for this: We use sugar as our main spice. A pity, when there are so many others that provide a better flavor. This is for 2 people.

2 whole sweet potatoes
1 whole apple
2 Tbl margarine or butter
1/2 tsp nutmeg
1/2 tsp cinnamon

1. Peel sweet potatoes and slice them lengthwise about 1/2 inch thick. Slice the apple into rings equally thick.

2. Grease the container—either a covered casserole-style container or aluminum foil—with margarine or butter.

3. Sprinkle spices lightly on both sweet potato and apple. Alternate slices of sweet potato and apple, with the sweet potato at the top and bottom.

4. Cook wrapped in foil on a grill for about 1 hour, or 50 minutes in a covered container in the oven at 350°F (180°C), until potato is tender. The key is not to dry out either the potato or the apple.

MARINATED SNAP BEANS

1 1/2 lbs fresh snap beans or canned green beans
2 garlic cloves, minced
4 Tbl olive oil
1 Tbl wine vinegar
1 Tbl lemon juice
2 Tbl chopped tarragon

1. For fresh beans, trim ends of beans and leave whole. Steam them for 3–4 minutes, until tender. Drain beans and rinse with fresh water. For canned green beans, simply open the can and drain.

2. Mix remaining ingredients, except tarragon, in bowl. Add beans and coat them with dressing.

3. Add tarragon. Place bowl in cooler to chill.

CANDIED CARROTS

You can always use artificial sweetener in place of the sugar. This is one vegetable you'll probably have to hide from the kids. Serves 4–6.

6–8 medium carrots
1/4 cup sugar
1/4 cup orange juice
1/2 cup water
1/4 tsp ground cinnamon
2 tsp cornstarch

1. Peel and slice carrots. Place remaining ingredients, except cornstarch, in pan or pot and boil for 20 minutes or until tender.

2. Add cornstarch and cook 10 minutes longer.

SPICY-HONEYED SWEET POTATOES

This tastes good enough to be a dessert. Backpackers will want to make this ahead of time to cut down on baggage. Serves 4.

4 or 5 medium sweet potatoes
1/8 cup melted margarine or butter (or olive oil)
3/4 cup honey or maple syrup
1/2 tsp ground cinnamon
1/4 tsp ground nutmeg

1. Cook sweet potatoes in boiling water (or wrapped in foil on grill) for 30 minutes or until tender. Peel potatoes and slice them 1/2 inch thick.

2. Mix together nutmeg, cinnamon, honey/maple syrup, and margarine. Layer potatoes in buttered cooking dish and pour sauce over each layer. Baste potatoes with sauce several times and bake 30–35 minutes, until glazed.

BROCCOLI WITH HERBS

Another easy vegetable to pack around for a day or two without refrigeration. This serves 4.

1 bunch of broccoli
2 cups water
2 chicken bouillon cubes
1 small onion, chopped
1 tsp marjoram or oregano
1 tsp basil
2 Tbl olive oil

1. Cut off the stalk ends and any large leaves. Lengthwise, cut thick stalks in half.

2. Dissolve bouillon cubes in a skillet with 2 cups of water. Then add all other ingredients, including broccoli, and simmer, covered, for 10 minutes or until tender.

3. Drain and add a small amount of margarine before serving.

TOFU IN BBQ SAUCE

Also called bean curd, tofu is actually curdled soybean milk that is rich in protein, with only a modest number of calories. Vegetarians often use it as a meat substitute. Like James Bond, tofu blends in well with everything and actually takes on different flavors, depending on how it is prepared. Most store-bought tofu is tofu mixed with a little water, known as soft tofu. The Japanese prefer this type, while the Chinese like their tofu more firm. This recipe serves 6. It's best served over bread, like an open-faced sandwich.

1 lb tofu
1 Tbl minced garlic
1 Tbl chopped onion
2 Tbl cooking oil
1 cup your favorite BBQ sauce

1. Slice tofu into 1-inch slices.

2. Saute onion and garlic in cooking oil. Add tofu and BBQ sauce.

3. Cook over medium heat for 8–10 minutes to allow tofu to acquire BBQ flavor.

CLASSIC SPANISH RICE

Many good rice mixes are on the market today, but there's something very satisfying about making your own; for one thing, the ingredients are a lot fresher. This serve 5–6.

1 cup raw rice
1/3 cup olive oil
1 onion, finely chopped
1/4 cup sweet red pepper
1/4 cup sweet green pepper
2 cups chicken bouillon
1/2 cup grated Parmesan cheese
Hot sauce to taste

1. Saute onion and peppers in olive oil and cook until all are limp.

2. Add rice and stir thoroughly while cooking. Once the rice turns yellow, add bouillon and simmer, covered, for 20 minutes.

3. Add the cheese and continue cooking until all the liquid is gone. Do not allow rice to become mushy. Allow folks to add their own hot sauce.

MEXICAN MUSHROOMS

This is a good side dish for many entrees. Either fresh or canned mushrooms can be used. You also have the choice about how hot you want this to be, depending on your chili powder selection. This serves 6–8.

2 lbs mushrooms
4 Tbl olive oil
2 Tbl minced garlic
4 Tbl regular chili powder or hot Mexican chili powder

1. Clean, drain, and dry mushrooms. Saute the garlic in olive oil for about a minute.

2. Add mushrooms and chili powder in that order. Cook, covered, for a few minutes, until mushrooms are tender.

NUTTY BROCCOLI AND CAULIFLOWER

This dish, actually a type of crumble, is a complete vegetarian meal that requires the services of both a skillet and an oven. Serves 4.

2 Tbl olive oil
1 small onion, chopped
1 cup broccoli florets
1 cup cauliflower florets
2 Tbl plain flour
1/2 pint skim milk
4 oz grated cheddar cheese
Pinch of nutmeg

Topping
8 Tbl plain flour
4 Tbl butter or margarine
1 tsp powdered mustard
4 oz chopped walnuts
Pinch cayenne pepper

1. In a skillet, heat the olive oil and saute the onion until soft, about 3–4 minutes. Add broccoli and cauliflower and cook for 5 minutes.

2. To the skillet, add the flour, then stir in the milk. Bring to a boil and cook for 5 more minutes, until everything begins to thicken.

3. Remove skillet from fire. Stir in nutmeg and half the shredded cheddar cheese. Pour into a 1-quart baking dish.

4. Now prepare the topping. Put the flour and butter into a bowl and mix until it is the texture of coarse breadcrumbs. Add the cayenne pepper, the dry mustard, the walnuts, and the rest of the cheddar cheese. Sprinkle this mixture over the vegetables.

5. Bake in a hot oven until topping is brown, about 15–20 minutes.

AVOCADO PASTA

An unusual, meatless way to serve noodles. It beats macaroni and cheese anytime, especially in summer. Serves 4.

1-lb box of pasta
1 avocado pear
1 cup yogurt
1 tsp coriander
1 green chili, seeded and finely chopped
1 Tbl lime juice

1. Begin cooking pasta.

2. Drain yogurt and place in a bowl. Mash in the peeled avocado and the rest of the ingredients.

3. Once the noodles are finished, mix them with the avocado and serve immediately.

SPICY FRIED POTATO ROLLS

Like fried potatoes but sick of French fries? These potatoes have incredible taste. Serves 4.

6–8 medium potatoes
1 Tbl coriander
1 medium onion, finely chopped
1/2 tsp ground ginger
1/4 tsp crushed green chili (or wet jerk seasoning)
1 Tbl lemon juice
2 cups flour
Salt and pepper to taste
Cooking oil

1. Cook potatoes and mash. Add everything but flour and mix thoroughly.

2. From the potato mix, form about 20 balls of equal size.

3. To the flour, mix in enough water to create paste of medium consistency. It should not be runny like milk. Add salt and pepper to taste.

4. Heat the oil hot enough for deep-frying (medium heat is fine, since everything is already cooked). Dip each potato ball into the flour and add it to the frying pan. Cook until a golden brown.

CAJUN FRIES

Another alternative to boring French fries. These can be addictive; you definitely won't be able to eat just one. Serves 4.

6–8 medium potatoes
2 cups plain flour
1 cup water
4 Tbl cayenne pepper
1 Tbl garlic salt
2 Tbl paprika (optional)
Cooking oil

1. Peel potatoes and slice into fry-sized strips. Heat the cooking oil over a hot fire.

2. Mix flour, spices, and water into a runny batter. Dredge potatoes through batter and fry until potatoes are tender. Drain on paper towels. Serve hot.

SPICY SPINACH

Too bad Popeye didn't know about this recipe. He might have taken the time to cook his spinach instead of chugging it out of a can. Serves 4.

2 15-oz cans of spinach
1 medium onion, finely chopped
1 Tbl minced garlic
2 tsp ground coriander
1 green chili, seeded and chopped
1/2 tsp ground ginger
1 tsp ground cumin
1 tomato
2 Tbl cooking oil

1. Drain spinach well. Chop finely. Slice the tomato.

2. Meanwhile, in a skillet, saute onion in oil until it is limp. Add the chili and spices and cook for 1 minute.

3. Add the chopped spinach and sliced tomato. Cook over low heat for about 6 minutes. Cook away any excess liquid.

REFRIED BEANS
WITH PICANTE-STYLE VEGGIES

Amazingly, I found this dish in England. Serves 3–4.

2 16-oz cans fat-free refried beans
1 16-oz can corn
1 cup broccoli
1 cup medium picante sauce
1/2 cup grated cheese (optional)

1. In a skillet, cook broccoli and corn together in corn juice until both are just tender. Drain and remove vegetables.

2. In the same skillet, warm the refried beans. Add broccoli and corn. Pour picante sauce and cheese over vegetables. Heat the contents thoroughly and serve.

CHAPTER SEVEN

Appetizers

SHRIMP COCKTAIL

Ever notice that some shrimp cocktails are delicious, while others are bland concoctions that seem to have all the zest of an octogenarian? This shrimp cocktail is guaranteed to be one of the memorable ones. It's as much a salad as a shrimp cocktail. Serves 8.

2 lbs cooked and peeled shrimp
1 large onion, diced
1 large cucumber, diced
1 large tomato, diced
4 lettuce leaves, cut in julienne
Cocktail sauce (catsup with prepared horseradish)

1. In a small bowl for each person, place the lettuce at the bottom. Add the vegetables on top of the lettuce.

2. Cut the shrimp in half lengthwise. Place enough shrimp to cover the vegetables. Pour a little of the cocktail sauce over the shrimp. Garnish with a single shrimp and a slice of lemon.

BABA GHANOUSH

A light appetizer that owes its origins to the Middle East, where it is a staple. A blender is needed to mix things thoroughly, so prepare this one in advance at home.

1 1/2 lb eggplant
1/4 cup parsley flakes
1/2 cup walnuts (toasted pine nuts are even better)
3 Tbl lemon juice
3 Tbl plain nonfat yogurt
6 Tbl olive oil
1 tsp salt
2 tsp minced garlic

1. Cook eggplant in 400°F (200°C) oven for 30 minutes. Remove from oven, cut in half, and scoop out the flesh.

2. Mash inside of eggplant with lemon juice until smooth. Mash salt and garlic together and add to eggplant.

3. Add yogurt to eggplant. Let cool. Then add nuts and parsley. Just before serving, drizzle with olive oil.

4. Serve as a dip with triangles of pita bread, or even tortilla chips.

HERB SPREAD

Can be used as a spread for crackers or warm French bread, and can be prepared at home ahead of time.

1 Tbl minced garlic
1/4 cup chives
1/2 cup sweet basil leaves
1/4 cup chopped pitted olives, black or green
8 oz nonfat cream cheese
1/4 cup parsley flakes

1. Mix garlic and herbs together, smoothing as much as possible.

2. Add cream cheese and mix until smooth.

3. Add chopped olives. Chill.

ARTICHOKE HEARTS
WITH ROQUEFORT DRESSING

Technically, this could probably fit under the salad category, too, but we're viewing it as an appetizer.

1 6-oz can artichoke hearts
1 wedge Roquefort cheese (bleu would work, too)
3 Tbl olive oil
1 tsp lemon juice

1. First, crumble the cheese. In a pan, warm the olive oil, lemon juice, and cheese.

2. Pour mixture over artichoke hearts or allow people to dip their own from individual containers.

CHILIES CON QUESO

You can make your own chilies and cheese at camp. You can control the heat of this dish by the salsa you use. Serves 5–6.

3/4 lb chopped cheddar cheese
1 Tbl hot salsa
6 poblano chilies or any small sweet green pepper—not hot ones unless you really like things hot
1/2 cup flour
3 eggs
3 Tbl Italian bread crumbs
Oil for frying
Hot sauce to taste

1. In each whole pepper, make a small hole and remove seeds and veins.

2. Mix cheese and salsa. Roll cheese into long strips and stuff a few ounces into each pepper. You may need toothpicks to keep the cheese sealed inside the pepper.

3. Beat eggs while adding 5 Tbl of flour, one Tbl at a time. In the remaining flour, roll each pepper.

4. Dip peppers into egg mix and roll in bread crumbs. Fry over medium-high heat until peppers turn brown. Serve hot, allowing folks to add their own hot sauce.

CHILIES, CHEESE, AND HAM

So simple and so good. In just 5 minutes, you can have everything ready and let everyone assemble their own.

20 1/2-inch cubes of cheddar cheese
20 1/2-inch cubes of cooked ham
20 small cubes of hot pepper
Box of toothpicks
Pineapple cubes (optional)
Hot sauce to taste (optional)

On a toothpick, place a cube of ham, a slice of pepper, and a cube of cheese. Add optional items if desired.

GREEK-STYLE MEATBALLS

People expect hamburgers on a camping trip, but certainly not meatball appetizers. Makes about two dozen meatballs.

1 lb lean hamburger
1/3 cup bread crumbs
1 egg
1/4 cup water
1 tsp prepared mustard
1/2 tsp allspice
1/2 tsp cinnamon
1/4 tsp ground cloves
1 tsp Worcestershire sauce
1/2 tsp oregano
1 tsp parsley flakes
1 tsp garlic salt
Toothpicks

1. Mix hamburger with all the spices. Make 1-inch meatballs.

2. Bake meatballs for about 20 minutes in 450°F oven. Drain on paper towels. Serve with toothpicks.

DOGS ON A STICK

Here's a good way to spice up hot dogs for a quick appetizer. Serves 4–6.

1-lb package of hot dogs (frankfurters or Vienna sausages)
2 Tbl prepared mustard
2 Tbl red currant jelly
3 Tbl cooking oil
Toothpicks

1. Cut the dogs into 1-inch pieces. Saute them in oil until they turn brown. Add mustard and red currant jelly.

2. Stir franks until they are thoroughly coated. Add more mustard and red currant jelly if necessary.

3. Once they are coated with a sticky glaze, remove them from the heat and place in a warm serving dish. Have the toothpicks handy for spearing.

PIZZA ROLLS

Use hot dog rolls for this easy and very tasty snack. Add pepperoni, sliced green peppers, sliced onion, and oregano, and this could make a complete meal. Serves 4.

4 hot dog rolls
4 Tbl tomato paste or catsup
1 Tbl soft butter
1 tsp sugar
1/4 cup sliced cheddar cheese
1/4 cup grated Parmesan cheese
2 large tomatoes
Pinch of oregano
Aluminum foil for baking over fire

1. Slice the hot dog rolls in half lengthwise (or, if they are sliced, simply separate them). Scoop out a small part of each hot dog roll, also lengthwise.

2. Mix the butter, tomato paste, sugar, oregano. Using a spoon, place some of mixture in the hollow of each roll.

3. On top of the mix, place cheese strips, a slice of tomato, and a sprinkle of Parmesan cheese. If an oven is available, place rolls in oven dish and bake uncovered until the cheese is soft and brown, about 20–25 minutes.

4. For preparing over an open fire, place rolls, bottomside down, on a sheet of aluminum foil. Place another sheet on top and loosely seal at the edges. Place on moderate fire for 10–15 minutes, until cheese is soft and hot.

ANCHOVY DIP

This is for the anchovy lover, of which I am not one. My anchovy-loving friends swear by this recipe, which requires a blender or a great deal of hand mixing, so it ought to be made ahead of time.

1 can anchovies
3 oz drained capers
1 14-oz can black olives drained and stoned
1 Tbl basil leaves
2 Tbl olive oil
2 tsp lemon juice
1 Tbl minced garlic
Ground pepper to taste
Crackers

1. Mash olives and capers together and stir until mixture is almost a liquid. Add all other ingredients except crackers, including the oil from the anchovy can, and blend into a paste.

2. Serve with crackers or crusty slices of bread.

CHAPTER EIGHT

Stir-Fry

Stir-fry is not a method normally associated with camp cooking, but it certainly should be. While stir-frying may require a little bit more time chopping vegetables, it normally requires far less fuel than other types of cooking—an important consideration when you're on an extended trip or backpacking.

Stir-fry, the Asian version of fast food, will probably become one of your favorite new ways to camp-cook. The first time you do it, you'll probably receive a lot of surprised looks. And a lot more appreciative glances when everyone first tastes it.

Further, this is often one of the healthiest ways to eat . . . as long as you use reduced-sodium soy sauce. Use regular soy sauce and you'll never have to take salt tablets again.

Note: If cooking fuel is at a premium, use Minute rice. Broccoli can be added to many of the Asian recipes if transporting it is possible.

For short trips, you will probably find it easier to prepare all the vegetables and spices at home, ahead of time, and carry them as a ready-mix in a resealable plastic bag.

CHICKEN AND RADISH STIR FRY

The cooking time is right, but this is too much stuff for backpackers to haul.

2 Tsp oil or butter
2 Tsp water
1 1/2 tsp cornstarch
3/4 cup water
1/2 tsp ground ginger
1 chicken bouillon cube
1 cup quartered radishes, trimmed
1 cup fresh broccoli florets or fresh green beans (in 1/2-inch cubes);
or 1/2 cup each of chopped bell pepper and onion
1 lb boneless, skinless chicken breasts in 1/2-inch strips
(or 1 12.5-oz can white chicken meat)
1 1/2 cup hoisin sauce
1 box oriental noodles

1. Heat the oil in the skillet until it is hot. Add the fresh vegetable of choice and stir to coat evenly with oil. Add the 2 tsp of water and cook food covered for about 3 minutes, until the vegetables are crisp/tender.

2. Mix cornstarch and 3/4 cup of water in a cup or bowl.

3. Add the chicken to skillet, stirring periodically for about 1 minute, until the meat is tender.

4. Add chicken bouillon cube, ground ginger, cornstarch mixture (step 2) and hoisin sauce. Stir constantly until mixture begins to boil (about 1 minute). Add radishes and cook and stir until mixture thickens (about 1 minute more).

5. Serve over oriental noodles.

BBQ CHICKEN

This recipe uses canned chicken rather than whole parts. A whole chicken could be baked at about 375°F (190°C) for an hour, or even grilled over indirect heat. For 2–3.

1 12.5-oz can white chicken meat
1/4 cup hoisin sauce
2 Tbl soy sauce
1 Tbl sugar
2 Tbl corn or safflower oil
1 Tbl minced garlic
1 Tbl ketchup
2 cups cooked rice

1. Prepare the rice first, since it will require the longest cooking time. Cook rice in a tightly covered container and let it stand for about 5 minutes after all the water has been absorbed.

2. While rice is cooking, drain chicken and mix together all ingredients except oil in a bowl. Let stand for 5–10 minutes.

3. In a skillet, add the 2 Tbl of oil and heat pan to very hot. Add the chicken and stir constantly over high heat for about 1 minute. Remove and serve over the steaming rice.

4. For a more complete meal, you may want to add slivers of carrots or broccoli to the chicken while it is cooking.

SPICY CHICKEN

This also works well with a whole roasted chicken, baked in an oven for almost an hour. Relying on canned chicken again makes it possible to serve this as a stir-fry.

2 12.5-oz cans cooked chicken
2–3 cups Minute rice
2 Tbl corn or safflower oil
1/2 tsp five-spice powder
1/2 tsp ground ginger
6 Tbl hoisin sauce
1/2 tsp soy sauce
3 sticks of carrots, slivered (optional)

1. Prepare rice. Meanwhile, marinate drained chicken with spices and sauces.

2. Heat skillet and add oil for cooking. When pan is very hot, add all items and stir continually for about 1–2 minutes. Remove and serve over hot rice.

CHICKEN FAJITAS

Stir-fry isn't limited to Asia. This simple but tasty chicken fajita recipe works just as well with hamburger if you can pack it and keep it cool. You'll probably want to premix all the ingredients except the chicken in a sealable container. Serves 2–4.

2 12.5-oz cans cooked chicken
2 Tbl corn or safflower oil
4 oz cheddar cheese
1 small onion, chopped
Small jar of your favorite salsa
1/4 cup fajita sauce
4–6 soft flour tortillas
Hot sauce (optional)
Sliced bell pepper (optional)
1 16-oz can refried beans (optional)

1. Mix meat with fajita sauce and let sit for 15 minutes. Meanwhile, cut the cheese up into small pieces or strips so it can be added to the chicken once it is cooked. Begin to heat the refried beans separately.

2. Heat skillet and add cooking oil. Over high heat, cook optional bell pepper slices for 2 minutes. Add onion and cook until translucent. Add chicken and cook for 1 minute. Remove all ingredients to serving pan. If desired, whirl tortillas in pan briefly, just enough to warm.

3. Make individual fajitas with tortillas, adding cheese, salsa and hot sauce. Serve with warm refried beans.

CHICKEN TOSTADAS

This is a modified version of the fajita recipe. It includes virtually the same ingredients; they're just arranged a little differently. This is a good, quick meal for those of us who like to mix our food. Serves 2–4.

2 12.5-oz cans cooked chicken
6 Tbl fajita sauce
2 Tbl corn or safflower oil
1 16-oz can refried beans
1 small onion chopped
4 oz cheddar cheese
Small jar favorite salsa or picante sauce
Hot sauce (optional)
Lettuce leaves (optional)
4–6 soft flour tortillas

1. Marinate chicken in fajita sauce. Warm up refried beans. Chop cheese into thin strips. Chop onions and lettuce.

2. In a hot pan, add cooking oil. Cook chicken for 1–2 minutes and remove.

3. On a plate, place a soft tortilla. Layer with refried beans, cheese, chopped raw onions, lettuce, and chicken, in that order. Add salsa and/or hot sauce.

CURRIED CHICKEN

Optional chili pepper flakes warm up this simple stir-fry for those who want their curry hot instead of simply flavorful. This is sort of an Asian version of the Italian classic, spaghetti, with curry taking the place of the tomato sauce. Real coconut milk is the preferred way to make this dish, but coconut milk is so full of fat it can't be recommended. Premix the ingredients in a resealable container, but leave the chicken canned until you start cooking. Serves 2–4.

2 12.5-oz cans cooked chicken (tuna canned in water works just as well)
1.5 Tbl curry powder
2 tsp imitation coconut extract
2 Tbl corn or safflower oil
1/4 tsp chili pepper flakes (optional)
1/2 tsp minced garlic
1 small onion, chopped
2 cups flat fettucine noodles
1 cup milk (real or powdered)
2 Tbl minced garlic

1. Prepare noodles separately. In a medium-hot pan, add oil for cooking. Add onions and cook until translucent. Add chicken, garlic, and optional chili peppers and stir continuously for about 30 seconds. Remove all ingredients and drain oil from pan.

2. Add milk, coconut extract, and curry powder to pan. Once milk is heated, return chicken, onions, and peppers to pan. Cook, stirring constantly, for about 2 minutes. Remove pan from fire and let sit for 5 minutes.

3. Spoon chicken over noodles. Use the curry and milk mix as your sauce.

CURRIED VEGGIES AND NOODLES

This flavorful dish uses the same basic ingredients but without the meat. Since the curry is providing all the real flavor, even die-hard carnivores may not notice that meat is missing. Any of your favorite vegetables should work. Serves 2–4.

2 cups milk
4 Tbl corn or safflower oil
2 Tbl curry powder
2 Tbl imitation coconut extract
3 Tbl shredded coconut (optional)
1/2 cup chopped bell pepper
1/2 cup shredded carrot
1/2 cup broccoli florets
1/4 cup chopped onion
2 Tbl minced garlic
2 cups fettucine noodles

1. Prepare noodles separately. In a hot pan, add cooking oil and broccoli florets. Cook, stirring constantly, for 2 minutes. Add bell pepper and garlic and cook for 1 minute. Add onion and carrots and cook for 1 minute more.

2. Remove all ingredients and place in a separate container. Drain all the liquid from the cooking pan. Add milk, curry, and coconut extract and heat liquid. Add vegetables, stir slowly for 1 minute over medium fire, and let stand for 2–3 minutes. Serve over cooked noodles. Sprinkle optional shredded coconut over each plate.

LEMON FRIED CHICKEN

This is a modified version of fried chicken that, once you try it, may have you making some important changes in how you cook your traditional fried chicken. The cornstarch produces a crispy light coating, whereas the usual flour coating tends to do little more than get soggy. Serves 2–4.

2 12.5-oz cans canned chunk chicken
3 Tbl soy sauce
2 Tbl minced garlic
2 tsp sesame oil
1/2 cup cornstarch
2 eggs
3 Tbl lemon juice
1/4 cup water
1 cup chicken bouillon
1 tsp cornstarch
1 tsp sugar (or substitute)
3 Tbl corn or safflower oil for cooking

1. Place chicken in a resealable plastic bag with soy sauce, minced garlic, and 1 tsp sesame oil. Let stand for 5 minutes.

2. In a bowl, lightly beat the eggs. Mix 1/2 cup cornstarch with 1/4 cup of water in a bowl.

3. If you have only one burner available, combine lemon juice, chicken bouillon, sugar, and remaining cornstarch and sesame oil in a saucepan and heat. Set this mixture aside, then heat the cooking oil in the frying pan. If you have two burners available, heat the cooking oil in the frying pan and use the second burner for heating the mixture of lemon juice, chicken bouillon, cornstarch, and sugar.

4. Drape chicken chunks through the egg and cornstarch, in that order. You may have to press the cornstarch onto the meat so that it sticks. Fry pieces of chicken for only 2–3 minutes. Placed cooked chicken on paper towel to drain until all meat is cooked.

5. Place lemon sauce in a bowl, cooked chicken on a plate. Use the sauce for dipping.

CHAPTER NINE

Soups and Stews

All of these can be made at home ahead of time and carried in a resealable plastic bag in an ice chest. What you don't need right away can be frozen.

FRENCH ONION SOUP

On a cold night, why wait until coffee to add the brandy? Serves 4–6.

1 tsp brandy
6 large onions
1/4 cup olive oil
32 oz (2 quarts) of water
4 beef bouillon cubes
1/4 cup butter or margarine
6 slices French bread
Grated Parmesan cheese
Salt & pepper to taste

1. Slice onions thinly and place in large pot. Cook slowly in olive oil until the onion is almost clear and tender.

2. Add butter, cover pot, and cook until onions no longer taste raw. Season with sprinkle of salt and pepper.

3. Add water and bouillon cubes and bring to boil. Simmer uncovered for 15–20 minutes.

4. In the meantime, butter and toast the bread slices on the grill.

5. When ready to serve, bring soup to boil again and add brandy. Add Parmesan cheese to bread and place each slice in the bottom of a bowl. Add soup, and sprinkle more cheese on the top.

EASY GUMBO

Gumbo is another of those items not normally found around a campfire, which makes it that much more of a treat. Hearty and flavorful, this will feed 4–6 people. Leftover sausage or chicken can also be used in place of the canned seafood.

1 bay leaf
1 Tbl Worcestershire sauce
2 cans cooked shrimp
1 can crabmeat
1 large onion, sliced
1 small green pepper, diced
8 oz canned tomatoes
1 tsp minced garlic
2 Tbl all-purpose flour
3 cups chicken bouillon
1/2 tsp thyme
2 Tbl margarine or olive oil
Hot sauce (to taste)
Crackers or bread (for dippin')

1. In a skillet, saute the onion and pepper in olive oil for about 5 minutes. Add flour and garlic. Stir.

2. Add chicken bouillon, tomatoes, thyme, bay leaf, Worcestershire, and salt and pepper to taste. Simmer about 1 hour.

3. Add shrimp and crabmeat. Cook for 2 minutes. Serve with crackers or bread. Let everyone add their own hot sauce.

FISH STEW

Except for frying, small fish like bluegills seem to offer few worthwhile cooking opportunities. However, they will also stew quite nicely. This recipe, which requires almost an hour's worth of fuel, serves 4. Oh yes: You can make a fine fish broth in place of the 6 cups of water required for the recipe by simmering the fish head with a chopped onion for an hour.

1 lb fish fillets
2 Tbl lemon juice
3 medium potatoes
1 large onion, chopped
2 Tbl minced garlic
3 medium tomatoes (fresh or canned)
1/4 cup stuffed green olives
6 cups water
1 tsp oregano
1 Tbl olive oil
Salt and pepper to taste
Hot sauce to taste

1. In a large cooking container, saute the onion and garlic for just 2–3 minutes. Add water, oregano, and potatoes and simmer for 20 minutes or until potatoes are almost cooked.

2. Sprinkle lemon juice over fish and add to broth. After 5 minutes, add tomatoes and olives. Simmer for 5 more minutes. Serve.

BEEF PEANUT STEW

No kid, regardless of age, can pass up peanut butter, especially when it's part of the main course. Serves 8.

1 lb cubed stew beef
1/4 cup peanut butter
1/2 tsp powdered nutmeg
1 Tbl chili powder
4 medium onions, sliced
2 Tbl oil
1 Tbl flour
1 tsp minced garlic
1 pt water
1 red pimiento, chopped
2 Tbl tomato paste or catsup

1. Brown beef cubes with 1 Tbl oil, flour, chili powder, and nutmeg. After the meat is browned, add the rest of the ingredients except peanut butter. Simmer covered for 1 to 1 1/2 hours or until meat is tender.

2. During the last half hour, warm up peanut butter over low heat. Mix with 1 Tbl oil. Heat for 5 minutes. Add gradually to stew and simmer for the last 25 minutes.

CABBAGE SOUP

Cabbage soup is easy to make, filling, and quite delicious. This yields 4 servings.

1/2 cabbage, diced
1 1/2 pts water with 2 cubes chicken bouillon
2 oz sliced pepperoni
2 tsp parsley flakes
2 carrots, diced
1 Tbl olive oil
1 Tbl flour
1 tsp dry jerk seasoning (optional)
Salt and pepper to taste

1. Saute onion and carrots in olive oil until onions are wilted. Add cabbage and parsley. Simmer for 5 minutes.

2. Blend in flour and cook another 2–3 minutes. Then add chicken bouillion and dry jerk seasoning and mix thoroughly. Simmer 20–25 minutes.

3. Add pepperoni slices, salt, and pepper. Simmer another 5 minutes. Serve.

FAST BEEF SOUP

This is a fast, hearty meal with bread or sandwiches. Serves 4–6.

1 10 1/2-oz can condensed beef noodle soup
1 10 1/2-oz can condensed vegetable soup
1/4 cup red wine (optional)
8 oz sliced mushrooms
2 Tbl Tabasco Sauce
Black pepper to taste

1. Prepare soup according to directions on can. Mix.

2. Add mushrooms, wine, black pepper, and Tabasco. Heat and serve.

HUNGARIAN GOULASH SOUP

Paprika is more sweet than hot, so don't be bashful about using it. This classic soup serves 4–6.

8 oz stewing beef
2 Tbl olive oil
1 onion, chopped
1/4 tsp marjoram
2 tsp paprika
1 tsp minced garlic
2 Tbl flour
1 quart beef bouillon
2 cooked potatoes, diced
Hot sauce (optional)

1. Saute beef and onions in the olive oil. Once the meat is browned, add the paprika, marjoram, and garlic and mix well.

2. Add flour and beef bouillon and stir thoroughly. Simmer, covered, for 25 minutes.

3. Add potatoes and simmer 5 more minutes.

APPLE AND BREAD SOUP

This can be served either hot or cold and can be prepared well ahead of time. Served cold at lunch on a hot summer day, it's wonderful. Just about any fruit—cherries, strawberries—can be used to make a variation of this German dish. Serves 3–4, fewer if served really hot.

6 large cooking apples
1 Tbl seedless raisins
1 tsp cinnamon
1 tsp lemon juice
4 slices wheat bread
1 Tbl sugar
1 1/2 pts water

1. Soak bread in water, squeeze dry, and place in cooking pan. Peel and dice apples and add to bread.

2. Add water and simmer until apples are soft; do not discard water. Mash apples and bread; strain through a sieve if possible.

3. Return apple/bread pulp to the saucepan. Add cinnamon, raisins, and sugar. Reheat mixture.

4. Add lemon juice. Simmer 5 minutes. Serve hot or cold.

CURRIED CHICKEN NOODLE SOUP

Chicken soup is said to have many amazing healing properties, which could only be amplified by the addition of curry. The following recipe makes a gallon. You may want to prepare this soup ahead of time and freeze what you don't need immediately.

1 whole chicken, quartered
4 large carrots, sliced
3 celery stalks, sliced
2 large onions, cut into wedges
1 Tbl sage
1 tsp white pepper
2 Tbl parsley
3 Tbl curry powder
6 chicken bouillon cubes
8-oz package egg noodles

1. Remove skin from chicken. Fill 2/3 of a gallon-sized pot with water, add the 6 boullion cubes, and bring to a simmer. Add chicken.

2. Simmer until meat begins to fall away from the bones. Remove the chicken and immediately add carrots, celery, and onions. While vegetables are cooking, remove the chicken from the bones and cut into chunks.

3. When vegetables are just becoming tender, add egg noodles to the stock and bring to a boil until noodles are cooked. Return chicken to stock; once chicken is warm, dish up and serve.

LAMB STEW

Tasty, filling, and simple to prepare. Makes enough to feed 2, with leftovers for lunch.

2 lb boned shoulder lamb
1 Tbl oil
2 Tbl minced garlic
3 Tbl flour
2 beef bouillon cubes
3/4 pt water
8 oz peeled tomatoes
2 bay leaves
2 celery sticks (optional)
1/2 lb carrots, sliced
1 15-oz can of peas
1 Tbl parsley leaves
1 Tbl salt
2 large onions, sliced
Dash of thyme
1 Tbl Tabasco Sauce
Black pepper to taste

1. Cut meat into 1-inch cubes. Mix flour, salt, and pepper and coat meat with it. In the 1 Tbl of oil, brown the meat in a large pot.

2. Dissolve bouillon cubes in 3/4 pint of boiling water. Add to stew pot, along with garlic, tomatoes, bay leaves, and celery. Bring to a boil and simmer for 30 minutes.

3. Add sliced carrots, parsley, sliced onions, peeled tomatoes, dash of thyme, and Tabasco Sauce. Cover and simmer for 30–40 minutes, until meat is tender.

CHAPTER TEN

Salads

Salads are one thing people never expect on a camping trip. Even the most mundane tossed salad becomes something special when it's served on a paper plate. Here are a few unusual salads that are usually pretty easy to pack in, assuming the items will be eaten the first day.

CAESAR SALAD WITH BLACKENED CHICKEN

This is kind of a trendy dish, but the tastes are so good it will probably remain an all-time favorite. Nothing could be simpler to prepare. For 2.

1/2 head Romaine lettuce
Parmesan cheese
1/4 cup Caesar salad croutons
6-oz can cooked chicken meat (2 cans for a meal)
2 Tbl blackening or Cajun seasoning
1 Tbl olive oil
Caesar salad dressing (your favorite)

1. In a warm skillet, mix olive oil and blackening or Cajun seasoning. Drain canned chicken and add. Cook over low heat, tossing frequently.

2. In a bowl, tear lettuce into pieces. Add Caesar salad dressing (as much as you normally would add) and mix thoroughly. Add croutons and sprinkle liberally with Parmesan cheese.

3. Add warm seasoned chicken to the top of the salad. To make this meal really stand out, serve on paper plates. Some people will appreciate the incongruity.

BEET AND WALNUT SALAD

A good one to make ahead of time, since the longer the ingredients mix, the better.

2–3 beets cooked and peeled, or 16 oz canned beets
2 tart apples
1/2 cup feta cheese
1/2 cup shelled walnuts
1/4 cup vinaigrette dressing
2 Tbl parsley
1/2 head of lettuce

1. Beets and apples should be cubed the same size.

2. Mix them together in bowl with all other ingredients until everything is coated.

3. Chill or serve immediately over your favorite lettuce.

RUMANIAN SALAD

Here's an easy salad without the dressing. It makes a very filling lunch by itself. I first tasted this in Romania and was amazed how well all the flavors blend together. Serves 4.

1 large tomato
1 large bell pepper
4 wedges of cheese (your choice)
1 lb of pepperoni

1. Cut tomato, bell pepper, and pepperoni into 4 sections. Serve one of each with a wedge of cheese.

2. In eating, alternate each item. Otherwise, this is pretty bad.

MOCK LOBSTER SALAD WITH GINGER

You can either use tofu or imitation crab or lobster chunks carried in many grocery stores. Both of the imitations are actually fish.

1 lb firm or extra-firm tofu or imitation lobster meat
2 celery ribs, minced
1/2 tsp ground ginger
1 Tbl fresh dill
1 tsp paprika
1 tsp hot pepper sauce
1/2 cup fat-free mayonnaise

1. If using tofu, rinse and crumble it. For imitation lobster and crab, separate the chunks.

2. Mix all the ingredients together in a bowl. Then add tofu or imitation lobster meat and stir gently in order not to break the "lobster" up. Chill before serving.

CHAPTER ELEVEN

Grilled Main Courses

Once the fire is up and ready, this is perhaps the easiest and most satisfying way to cook outdoors. Best of all, there are no cooking utensils to clean.

Note: Make the marinades at home before leaving, and your steak, chicken, or ribs will be perfect when you arrive. This will also help cut down on the amount of spices and seasonings you'll need to pack.

JERK CHICKEN I

If you've never had this before, you are in for one of the treats of your life. I eat it at least once or twice a month because it's spicy and nothing could be simpler to prepare.

1 whole chicken, cut up
3 Tbl jerk marinade (see Chapter 4) or prepared wet jerk seasoning
Apple cider vinegar

1. Parboil chicken pieces in 2/3 water and 1/3 apple cider vinegar for 20 minutes. Place chicken on a platter and discard the liquid. Remove chicken skin and marinate with jerk for at least 30 minutes.

2. Grill over low or indirect heat for 20–25 minutes. Chicken should just be turning crispy but not overcooked.

JERK CHICKEN II

If you have only a fire and no way to parboil, this is a better approach, because this way the chicken doesn't dry out.

6 chicken legs
4 Tbl dry jerk seasoning (see Chapter 4)
1/2 cup olive oil
1 cup apple cider vinegar

1. Mix the olive oil, the apple cider vinegar, and half of the dry jerk seasoning in a resealable plastic bag. Remove all excess fat from the chicken and marinate it in the jerk sauce for 30 minutes.

2. Grill the chicken about 20 minutes each side. Add the remaining dry jerk to any leftover marinade for basting chicken while it is cooking.

GRILLED CHICKEN BREAST SWEET AND SOUR

The following recipe is incredibly easy and very tasty. Serves 2.

2 boneless chicken breasts marinated in soy sauce and pineapple juice (half and half)
2 pineapple rings (optional)

Cook marinated boneless chicken breast on grill for 3 minutes each side. Add pineapple rings and cook for 2 minutes. Goes well with rice pilaf or cole slaw.

INDIAN-STYLE MARINATED CHICKEN

This a tandoori-style recipe based on India's popular and spicy way of cooking. This is tasty, not hot, unless you use hot curry. Serves 3–6. If this calls for too many ingredients, try the simpler version that immediately follows this recipe.

6 chicken breasts or legs
1 small onion, minced
1 piece fresh ginger root (about 1 inch), minced
1 lemon
1 cup plain nonfat yogurt
2 tsp curry powder
1 tsp ground turmeric
1 tsp ground cumin
1 tsp ground coriander
1/2 tsp salt
1/4 tsp ground cardamom
    (continued)

1/4 tsp ground cloves
1/4 tsp ground cinnamon
1/4 tsp black pepper
1/4 tsp ground red pepper

1. Mix all ingredients in large resealable plastic bag. Add chicken and mix to coat it thoroughly. Refrigerate 4 hours, turning bag and chicken several times.

2. Cook on grill, using indirect heat if at all possible. Cooking time should be 35–45 minutes, depending on fire. Serve immediately.

EASY SPICY CHICKEN

This uses the same yogurt-style marinade as above, but then the ingredient list shortens drastically. *Marinate at least 1 hour.*

1 cut-up chicken or 4 chicken legs
1 cup plain nonfat yogurt
1 Tbl minced garlic
1/2 tsp ground ginger
1 tsp chili powder (or cut in half)
1/4 tsp ground cloves
1/2 tsp ground cinnamon

1. Parboil the chicken in 2/3 water and 1/3 apple cider vinegar, if possible, to reduce cooking time. Prepare all of the above ingredients for the marinade.

2. After parboiling, remove chicken skin and marinate meat for 1 hour. Cook over medium-low heat for about 20 minutes, basting frequently with leftover marinade.

CHICKEN WITH ROSEMARY BUTTER

A flavorful variation of grilled chicken. Simple but very, very good. Serves 2.

1 whole chicken or 4 chicken legs
1/3 cup butter or margarine
2 Tbl rosemary leaves
1 Tbl minced garlic
Black pepper to taste

1. Split whole chicken in half or cut up into 4 pieces.

2. Mix all ingredients together. To cook with skin on, baste the bone side and place it face down on the grill. Cook for 15 minutes. Baste skin side and cook it face down on grill for 15–20 minutes. Beware of flare-ups.

3. To cook without skin, simply remove the skin and cook for the same length of time but baste chicken about every 5–10 minutes to keep it from drying out. Parboiling first will help reduce cooking time.

4. You can also cook the chicken without skin by wrapping individual chicken pieces in foil and basting them liberally before sealing.

CURRY AND HONEY-GLAZED CHICKEN

Perhaps the best way to cook this is using a whole chicken on an electric rotisserie. If you're at a campground with electrical hookups, your problems are solved. Otherwise, it's easier and faster to grill the pieces separately to reduce cooking time. However you fix this recipe, though, it's a knockout.

1 whole chicken or 4 chicken legs
2 Tbl curry powder
2 Tbl minced garlic
1/4 cup honey
1/4 cup orange juice
4 Tbl Tabasco Sauce

1. If cooking a whole chicken with a rotisserie, rub half the garlic, curry powder, and Tabasco onto the chicken. Cook for about an hour, then baste with honey and orange juice mixed together with the remaining Tabasco, curry powder, and garlic for another half hour.

2. If cooking on the grill, rub half the seasonings onto the legs or the whole chicken cut into quarters. Cook the chicken for 25–30 minutes, turning it at least once. Using the same basting mixture described above, cook the chicken for another 15–20 minutes, turning and basting at least twice on each side.

LONDON BROIL WITH MUSTARD MARINADE

2 lbs top round steak, trimmed of fat
2 Tbl Dijon mustard
2 Tbl olive oil
2 Tbl lemon juice
1 Tbl soy sauce
1 tsp Worcestershire sauce
2 garlic cloves, crushed
1/4 tsp ground ginger
1/2 tsp black pepper

1. Mix all ingredients in a resealable plastic bag and add the steak. Let soak in marinade for at least 30 minutes, turning the bag 2–3 times.

2. Remove steak from marinade but do not scrape off any excess. Grill steak until it reaches desired degree of doneness.

3. Any marinade left in bowl (and there may not be much) should be warmed and poured over the steak once it is done. Put steak on warm platter and let sit for 5 minutes before cutting. Slice into thin pieces and serve immediately.

COUNTRY-STYLE RIBS, VOLCANO-STYLE

This is both spicy and hot, but not overly so. Serves 6.

4 lbs country-style pork ribs
1 small onion, chopped
1 tsp minced garlic
1 Tbl cooking oil
1/3 cup apple cider vinegar
1/4 cup molasses
1 Tbl bottled hot sauce
2 tsp ground cayenne pepper
1 tsp chili powder
1/2 tsp salt
1 tsp Dijon mustard
1 1/2 cups catsup
Extra water and apple cider vinegar for parboiling

1. Parboil ribs in cooking pot and cover with 2/3 parts water and 1/3 parts

apple cider vinegar. Cook covered for 40 minutes.

2. While meat is parboiling, heat oil in skillet and cook onion and garlic until onion is tender and almost clear.

3. Add 1/3 cup apple cider vinegar, catsup, pepper sauce, cayenne pepper, chili powder, mustard, salt, and molasses. Bring skillet to boil, then simmer uncovered for about 15 minutes.

4. Baste ribs with mixture and grill over low fire for 30–40 minutes, turning and basting frequently. Indirect heat would also work well.

CLASSIC SHISH KEBABS

The secret to a good shish kebab, at least while camping, is not to mix meat and vegetables on the same skewer. The veggies take longer than the meat, and they cook at varying times. That's why the juicy, overdone tomatoes too often fall off and end up burning in the fire. The flavors get to mix together once everything is served on a plate. You can do a faster, easier version of this recipe by leaving out the tomato and bell pepper. Serves 4–6.

2 lbs sirloin or lamb
2 large onions
2 large tomatoes
2 bell peppers
1/2 cup wine vinegar
1/4 cup olive oil
1 tsp oregano leaves
1 tsp basil leaves
1/2 tsp black pepper
1 Tbl salt
1 Tbl minced garlic

1. Cut meat into 1-inch cubes. Slice bell pepper into 2-inch cubes. Peel onion and slice into wedges.

2. Mix all seasonings together in a plastic bag to form marinade. Place meat and vegetables in marinade for 1 hour.
3. Alternate meat and onions on the same skewer. Place bell peppers and

tomatoes on their own separate skewers. Put meat/onion and bell pepper over fire. Wait and put the tomatoes over the fire only during the last 5 minutes of cooking.

4. As the items finish cooking, you get to make the plates, putting everything together. If you let everyone do their own, the meat will probably disappear quickly.

PORK KEBABS WITH ARTICHOKE HEARTS

This is very different and not for those on a diet. But everyone deserves to treat themselves to marinated artichoke hearts every now and then. Serves 4.

1 lb boneless lean pork, cut into 1-inch cubes
1 6-oz jar of marinated artichoke hearts
1 green or red bell pepper, cut into 1-inch cubes
1 tsp hot pepper sauce
1/2 tsp oregano
1/2 tsp basil
2 Tbl lemon juice
2 tsp black pepper

1. Place pork cubes in resealable plastic bag. Drain in marinade from the artichoke hearts. Add pepper sauce, oregano, basil, lemon juice and black pepper. Mix well and let marinate for at least 30 minutes.

2. Place marinated pork, artichoke hearts, and pepper squares on metal skewers. Grill for 15–20 minutes.

HORSERADISH BURGERS

Looking for a variation of the same old burger? This works quite well, and most people will probably want seconds, so you may want to double the recipe. This makes 4 quarter-pound burgers.

1 lb lean ground beef
2 Tbl Worcestershire sauce
1 tsp garlic salt
2 Tbl prepared horseradish
1 tsp prepared mustard
1 small onion, finely chopped
1 egg

In a bowl or plastic bag, mix all ingredients together as if making a meat-loaf. Make 4 individual burgers and grill, turning once. You may want to offer more horseradish with any other toppings.

BURGERS WITH SPUDS

This begins to approach more of a meal, with the potatoes included as part of the burger. The curry makes this an American variation of the famous Indian sandwich known as a "roti." If you like your burgers rare, use potatoes that are already cooked. The following recipe makes 6 burgers.

1 lb ground beef
1/2 cup grated, peeled potatoes
1 tsp curry
1 egg

In a bowl, mix everything together thoroughly. Make 6 burger patties. Cook for 10–15 minutes, until the burgers are medium. Turn only once.

BURGERS WITH A BITE

This should satisfy those who like all their food hot. Add as much hot sauce as you like: Green Tabasco is a real eye-opener. The hot cheese on top is what really sets this off. Makes 4.

1 lb hamburger
6–8 drops of hot sauce
2 Tbl chopped onion
1 Tbl soy sauce
1 egg
1/4 cup dry cereal (or Italian bread crumbs)
4 hot pepper cheese slices

Mix all ingredients together except cheese. Place burgers on grill and cook until desired doneness, turning only once. Place the cheese on top after turning the patties.

HOT-N-SPICY CHEESEBURGERS

The problem with the traditional placement of cheese only on the top, as in the above recipe, is that there's very little hot cheese except on the top. This recipe remedies that. Makes 4 burgers.

1 lb ground chuck or ground round
1 cup grated hot pepper cheese
1 Tbl BBQ sauce
1 onion, chopped
1 Tbl garlic salt
Pepper to taste

1. Mix all ingredients in a bowl so that the cheese is spread throughout. However, if you are a real cheese lover, save a couple of slices to put on top, too.

2. Grill until desired doneness. Catsup and mustard and pickles, or BBQ sauce alone, make good toppings.

GARLIC RIBS

I like to parboil both chicken and ribs since the process removes much of the fat, makes the meat crisper, and cuts down on the grilling time. Grilling too long with any sauce containing a good amount of sugar is certain to char the meat. Save any leftover sauce for grilling chicken.

4–6 pounds pork ribs
1 tsp thyme leaves
2 tsp oregano leaves
2 tsp garlic salt
1 Tbl black pepper
Extra apple cider vinegar and water for parboiling

Sauce

2 tsp minced garlic
2 tsp black pepper
1 tsp prepared mustard
2 Tbl soy sauce
2 Tbl apple cider vinegar
1/4 cup your favorite steak sauce or Worcestershire
3 Tbl honey

1. Parboil ribs in liquid consisting of 2/3 water and 1/3 apple cider vinegar with thyme, oregano, garlic salt, and black pepper. Simmer for 10–15 minutes. Remove ribs to platter and discard liquid.

2. While ribs are parboiling, mix together all sauce ingredients. Baste ribs with sauce and let stand for 10 minutes. Grill over low or indirect heat, if possible. If direct heat must be used, try using a rib rack. Grill for 15–20 minutes, until ribs are crisp.

CHINESE-STYLE RIBS

The first step, parboiling, is the same as for the ribs above, but then the flavors take off in a whole new direction. Use same parboiling mixture as above.

Sauce

1/2 cup soy sauce
1/2 cup chili sauce
1 tsp ground ginger
2 tsp minced garlic
1 small onion, chopped

1. Parboil as in step 1 for Garlic Ribs.

2. Blend the sauce together in a bowl while the ribs are simmering. Baste ribs and cook over low heat until they are crisp.

CHAPTER TWELVE

Skillet Meals

Note: All the recipes call for margarine instead of butter. This is not a taste preference: Margarine is less likely to burn.

All sauces and marinades can be premixed at home and carried in resealable plastic bags.

STEAK WITH MUSTARD AND CAPER SAUCE

Capers are not used nearly enough in most cooking. What they add to a steak or grilled fish is wonderful. Use some tender cuts of meat here, the best steaks you can find. This recipe serves 4.

4 steaks
2 small onions, finely diced
2 Tbl wine vinegar
1/4 cup nonfat yogurt
1 Tbl Dijon mustard
2 Tbl drained and rinsed capers
2 Tbl margarine
6 Tbl beef bouillon mix
Dash of oregano

1. Put margarine in skillet. When it is sizzling, put steaks in pan and sear both sides quickly. Cook steaks to your liking, then set aside but keep warm.

2. In the same pan, add onion and wine vinegar. Cook until vinegar evaporates. Add bouillon, then yogurt. Simmer until mixture is reduced by almost half.

3. Remove skillet from heat. Add mustard and capers. Blend thoroughly, then pour over steaks. Add a sprinkle of oregano and serve.

CHICKEN DIJON

This can be made with either chicken breasts or chicken legs. It's a simple but very tasty variation on basic fried chicken.

6 chicken legs or breast halves
7 Tbl all-purpose flour, divided
1 tsp ground black pepper
2 Tbl margarine
2 Tbl olive oil
2 1/2 Tbl Dijon mustard
1 cup plain yogurt
1/4 tsp oregano
3/4 cup white wine

1. Heat margarine in skillet. Coat chicken with mixture of 4 Tbl flour and black pepper. Cook chicken on both sides for about 25 minutes or until golden brown. Make sure there are no red juices at the joints. Place chicken on platter.

2. Pour the other 3 Tbl of flour into the heated skillet and mix with juices, stirring until everything is blended and the liquid is simmering. Stir in mustard, wine, yogurt, and oregano. Stir continually until mixture begins to thicken.

3. Return chicken to skillet and cook over low heat for another 3–5 minutes to baste chicken well. Put chicken on platter and pour over the remaining sauce.

FRIED JERK CHICKEN

The meat will fall off the bone when this has finished cooking, and you may fall off your camp stool once you taste it. You should either cover the skillet or use a Dutch oven.

1 chicken, cut up and skin removed
1 cup water
4 tsp dry jerk seasoning or 2 tsp jerk paste (see Chapter 4)
2 onions, chopped
2 Tbl rum or rum extract
1/2 cup soy sauce

Combine all spices in the skillet and bring to a boil. Add the chicken. The liquid should just barely cover the chicken. Bring to a boil again, then cover and simmer for 20 minutes, turn the chicken, and simmer for another 20.

CLAMS AND SHRIMP
WITH BEARNAISE SAUCE

1 lb canned or fresh clams
8 oz canned or fresh shrimp
2 Tbl margarine
1/3 cup minced onion
3/4 cup white wine vinegar
1/2 cup chicken bouillon
1/4 tsp tarragon leaves
1 Tbl Dijon mustard
1/2 cup plain nonfat yogurt
Salt and pepper to taste

1. Melt margarine in skillet over medium-hot fire. Drain and rinse clams and shrimp, pat dry, and add to skillet. Cook for about 1 minute. (Cook for 3–4 minutes if using fresh seafood.)

2. Put seafood in bowl and set aside. To skillet, add onion, vinegar, chicken bouillon, and dry tarragon. Boil uncovered until liquid is reduced to half a cup.

3. Pour mustard and yogurt in skillet. Bring again to a boil and cook until mixture reduces to about 3/4 cup.

4. Stir in seafood and season with salt and pepper. Add a sprinkle of tarragon leaves to the top of the mixture after it is served on each plate. This goes well with sliced potatoes, which will make their own excellent use of the bearnaise sauce.

HONEY-MUSTARD FISH

This is a nice delicate seasoning that complements even the most delicate fish without overpowering it. Depending on the fish, these can also make great sandwiches. Serves 3–4.

1 lb fish fillets
1 Tbl lime juice
1 Tbl light mayonnaise
2 tsp honey
2 tsp Dijon mustard
1 tsp dried dill
2 tsp olive oil

1. Blend together mayonnaise, lime juice, honey, mustard, and dill. Coat fish.

2. Heat the olive oil in a skillet. Cook about 4 minutes each side, until the fish flakes. Serve warm or cold.

SPICY/HOT SALMON BURGERS

These are a great change from burgers and require just a little more work to put together. Makes 4 salmon burgers.

1 14-oz can of salmon (pink is fine)
2 eggs
1/2 cup bread crumbs
3 Tbl dill
2 Tbl Tabasco sauce
3 Tbl prepared horseradish
1/2 tsp salt
1 Tbl margarine
1 Tbl olive oil
1 small onion, diced (optional)
2 cooked potatoes, peeled
1 Tbl blackening or Cajun season

Tabasco Mayonnaise
1/3 cup fat-free mayonnaise
2 tsp dill
1 Tbl Tabasco Sauce (or more if you want it really hot)

1. In a bowl, first mash the potatoes, then add 1/4 cup of the bread crumbs and the dill, Tabasco Sauce, horseradish, salmon, and salt. Stir everything together.

2. Make four 1/2-inch patties. Coat them with the remaining 1/4 cup of bread crumbs.

3. Heat margarine and olive oil in a skillet. Over a medium-high fire, cook the salmon burgers for about 4 minutes on each side. Turn them only once.

4. Prepare the Tabasco mayonnaise in a bowl. It's easy to make a hot and a mild version depending on the amount of Tabasco. Serve separately with the salmon cakes.

CURRIED SHRIMP

This is far more than just shrimp and curry. The fruit flavors make a pronounced change. Serves 4.

3 Tbl margarine or olive oil
1 large onion, chopped
1 tsp minced garlic
1 large apple, cored and diced
2 tsp curry powder
4 Tbl flour
1 Tbl lemon juice
2 1/2 cups chicken bouillon
1 tsp allspice
1 cup nonfat yogurt
1 tsp salt
2 cups cooked shrimp
1/2 cup seedless raisins
2 Tbl chutney
Hot chilies, chopped (optional, to make this more hot than spicy)
Chinese noodles
Pepper to taste

1. In a skillet, saute garlic, onion, and apple in olive oil for about 5 minutes. Add curry and flour and mix thoroughly.

2. Remove skillet from heat. Gradually add chicken bouillon, lemon juice, and allspice. Add yogurt. Mix well.

3. Return skillet to fire and cook until the mixture thickens. Add 1 tsp salt and pepper to taste. Add raisins and chutney (and optional chilies) and simmer for about 15 minutes. In the meantime, prepare Chinese noodles. Add the shrimp to the sauce for only the last 2 minutes.

4. Serve shrimp over noodles.

HOT WINGS

How hot these wings turn out depends on your selection of pepper sauce. Tabasco will make this a mouth-burner, while Crystal Sauce will be spicy and hot.

2 lbs chicken wings or drumsticks
Oil for frying
2 Tbl margarine
1/4 cup hot red pepper sauce
1/2 cup fat-free sour cream
1/4 cup mayonnaise or salad dressing, your choice
1 Tbl lime juice

1. Cut off and throw away wing tips. Cut wings at joints. Fry at 375°F (190°C) for 8–10 minutes, cooking as many as possible at one time. Place cooked wings in warm bowl and keep warm.

2. In a second skillet, melt margarine, stir in pepper sauce, and pour over wings. Thoroughly coat wings.

3. For a dipping sauce, mix sour cream, mayonnaise, and lime juice.

BLACKENED TUNA OVER PASTA

No fresh fish needed, just a can of solid white albacore tuna. Don't use the cheaper tuna, which doesn't taste nearly as good. This is a fast, easy recipe that will become one of your favorites the first time you try it. Serves 2.

1 6-oz can solid white tuna in spring water (not oil)
6 Tbl olive oil
1 Tbl leaf basil
1 small onion, thinly sliced
1 small bell pepper, cut into thin strips
Blackened (or Cajun) fish seasoning
1 8-oz box of thin spaghetti noodles

1. Begin boiling pasta. In a skillet, heat 4 Tbl of olive oil. Cook onion and bell pepper until tender. Add tuna and liberally season the top with blackening mix. Turn the tuna and season the other side. Cook tuna long enough to thoroughly heat it.

2. Place the drained noodles in a separate, preheated bowl containing 2 Tbl olive oil and the leaf basil. Mix to coat the noodles with the basil leaf.

3. Place the noodles on serving plates, then add the blackened tuna over pasta.

GINGER BEEF

I love anything with ginger. There isn't anything it doesn't taste good with. This is really a stir-fry, so make sure the skillet is large enough. This serves 4.

1 lb of steak (sirloin, flank, top round)
6 Tbl white wine (optional)
6 Tbl soy sauce
4 Tbl peanut oil
2 tsp minced garlic
3 Tbl minced ginger
2 onions, thinly sliced
1 bell pepper, thinly sliced
Cooked rice (4 cups)

1. Cut meat 1/8 inch thick and about 3 inches long. Marinate it in a non-aluminum container with wine and half of soy sauce for at least 30 minutes, more if possible. Save marinade and combine it with the other half of the soy sauce and wine.

2. In skillet, heat onion slices and garlic in oil until onions are transparent. Add bell pepper slices and cook for 2–3 more minutes. Remove all vegetables from the skillet.

3. Add ginger and the beef. Cook over high heat until meat is medium rare, about 3 minutes. Return the vegetables to the skillet and add the marinade. Stir everything thoroughly for 1–2 minutes. Serve over rice.

CURRIED FRIED FISH

Fish can be whole or filleted, however you wish to serve them. This serves 3.

1 lb fish fillets
2 Tbl curry
1 tsp garlic salt
1/2 cup flour
1/2 cup safflower or corn oil
Chutney

1. Mix curry, garlic salt, and flour. Coat fish with mixture.

2. In a skillet, heat up the oil. Brown fish over moderate heat for about 4 minutes on each side. Fish is done when it flakes on both sides.

3. Serve, accompanied by chutney.

JERK FRIED FISH

Turning up the heat now. You'll never go back to plain old fried fish. Too boring. This is my all-time favorite way to fry fish. This also serves 3.

1 lb fish fillets
2 Tbl dry jerk seasoning (see Chapter 4)
1/2 cup flour
1 tsp garlic salt
1/2 cup safflower or corn oil

1. As in the Curried Fried Fish recipe, coat the fish with a mix of flour, dry jerk seasoning, and garlic salt.

2. In a skillet, heat the oil and fry fish for about 4 minutes on each side. Goes well with BBQ Beans or anything else "wet."

SPICY STEAMED WHOLE FISH

You want to use a fish that's not too oily. Slicing, or scoring, the skin is important so the flavors will penetrate the fish. You'll need a rack to steam the fish properly; otherwise, you'll end up with boiled fish and the seasonings will probably be too strong. Serves 3.

1 1/2 lbs dressed fish (no head)
1/4 tsp garlic salt
1/2 tsp ground pepper
1/4 tsp powdered ginger
3 cups water
2 tsp pickling spices
1 small onion, chopped

1. Score the scaled sides and rub fish with ginger, pepper and garlic salt.

2. In a skillet, add the water, pickling spices, and onion. Place the fish on a rack so that it is above the liquid. Simmer and cover for about 30 minutes, or until fish flakes. There is no need to turn the fish, since the steam will cook both sides simultaneously.

JERK STEAMED WHOLE FISH

This is a very spicy and hot dish. You'll need an accompaniment that's "wet," to help kill the fire. Serves 3.

1 1/2 lbs dressed fish (no head)
1 tsp dry jerk seasoning (see Chapter 4)
1/4 tsp garlic salt
2 tsp wet jerk seasoning (see Chapter 4)
3 cups water
1 small onion, chopped

1. Score the sides of the scaled fish and coat with a mixture of the dry jerk seasoning and garlic salt.

2. In a skillet, add the water, wet jerk seasoning and onion. Place the fish on a rack above the liquid and steam, covered, for about 30 minutes. There is no need to turn the fish, since the steam will cook both sides simultaneously.

TUNA AND NOODLES

Use only the solid white tuna, not the inferior chunk kind. Serves 4.

2 6-oz cans of tuna in water
2 Tbl minced garlic
1 cup chopped green pepper
1 tsp dry jerk seasoning
1 small onion, chopped
2 Tbl flour
1 1/2 cups chicken bouillon
1/2 cup sliced olives
Oil for frying
1 8-oz package linguine noodles

1. In a skillet, saute onion, chopped green pepper, and minced garlic. Add flour and stir, cooking for 1 more minute.

2. Add chicken bouillon, dry jerk seasoning, and sliced olives. Stir regularly. In a separate container, begin boiling noodles.

3. After the sauce thickens, add tuna and simmer for another 3–4 minutes. Taste sauce. Add more dry jerk seasoning if needed.

4. Serve tuna and sauce over buttered noodles.

GREEK-STYLE SPAGHETTI

Very different from the Italian variety, with a whole riot of new flavors. They are so novel, in fact, you may want to try it the first time as a side dish rather than a main course. The strange taste you can't identify is the cloves. Serves 4.

1 lb lean hamburger
2 small onions, chopped
3 Tbl olive oil
1 Tbl minced garlic
1 6-oz can tomato paste
1/2 tsp ground cinnamon
1/4 tsp ground cloves
2 cups water
Salt and pepper to taste
Buttered noodles or macaroni

1. Saute garlic and onions in olive oil. Add hamburger and brown. Season to taste with salt and pepper.

2. Add tomato paste and water and bring to a boil. Add spices, then simmer for 30 minutes, allowing flavors to blend thoroughly.

3. Serve over buttered noodles or macaroni

ITALIAN-STYLE SPAGHETTI

Consumer Reports rated Hunt's Traditional Homestyle Spaghetti Sauce as the nation's best, and you'll probably agree. Serves 4.

2 27.5-oz cans of Hunt's Traditional Homestyle Spaghetti Sauce
1 lb lean hamburger
3 Tbl minced garlic
1 large green pepper, sliced
1 large onion, sliced
2 Tbl oregano
2 Tbl basil
8 oz thin spaghetti

1. Saute 1 Tbl oregano with hamburger. In a large cooking pot, pour in spaghetti sauce, pepper, onion, spices, and the sauteed hamburger.

2. Bring sauce to a boil, then lower to a simmer. Cook for at least 30 minutes, until onion and green pepper are wilted. The longer this cooks, the better the flavor.

3. Serve with thin spaghetti noodles.

CHICKEN AND EGGPLANT WITH RAISINS 🐾

This is a wonderful example of Middle Eastern cooking. The regular recipe calls for lamb, but the canned chicken works just as well. Serves 6.

2 12.5-oz cans of white chicken meat
1/2 tsp ground cinnamon
4 Tbl seedless raisins
2 onions, chopped
1 large eggplant, trimmed and cubed
2 Tbl minced garlic
1/4 tsp ground cloves
1/4 cup water
1 beef bouillon cube
6 tomatoes, skinned and quartered
4 Tbl olive oil
Salt and pepper to taste

1. In a skillet, saute onions and garlic in oil until soft. Add chicken and eggplant to frying pan. Heat the water and dissolve the bouillon cube. Add to cooking pot. Add tomatoes, cloves, and cinnamon.

2. Bring skillet to a boil. Add salt and pepper to taste. Add raisins and stir. Simmer, covered, stirring regularly and adding water if necessary, until eggplant is falling apart.

SPICY SHRIMP WITH ANGEL HAIR PASTA

Instead of the much pricier angel hair pasta, use either thin spaghetti or vermicelli, which cost almost 50 percent less. There is hardly any difference in the noodle size. Use fresh shrimp if possible, otherwise canned. Serves 4.

1 lb shrimp, deveined and without shells
2 tsp prepared horseradish (not the sauce)
2 tsp ground ginger
2 Tbl soy sauce
1/2 cup chopped onion
5 Tbl olive oil
1 tsp minced garlic
1 Tbl oregano
8 oz thin spaghetti

1. Mix all the spices except the onion and oregano in a large resealable plastic bag with 2 Tbl of the olive oil. Marinate shrimp in mixture for 15–30 minutes.

2. In the meantime, cook noodles and drain. In 2 Tbl olive oil, warm up noodles. Add oregano and mix thoroughly. Turn off heat but keep noodles warm.

3. In a skillet, saute the onion in 1 Tbl olive oil. When the onion is limp, add the marinated shrimp. Cook for only 4–5 minutes, until shrimp turns color.

4. Serve shrimp over noodles.

CHAPTER THIRTEEN

Oven Entrees

Once your dinner is in the oven, take a nap or go fishing. The worst thing you can do is keep checking an oven, since every time you open the door or lid, you may add as much as 5 or 10 minutes of cooking time. So resist that temptation until your nose and your watch both indicate that things should be close to ready. Note: All sauces and marinades can be prepared at home in resealable plastic bags.

CHICKEN BREAST WITH MUSTARD SAUCE

This recipe can easily be doubled, depending on the amount of chicken being cooked. Expect people to want seconds.

16 oz plain fat-free yogurt
2 Tbl Dijon mustard
6 whole chicken breasts (to serve 6)
Ground black pepper
1 tsp lemon juice
1/2 tsp ground nutmeg
Salt

1. Mix together all ingredients in a bowl or plastic bag. Remove skin from chicken.

2. Place chicken in an oven-proof glass container and bake at 375°F for 45–50 minutes, until done. (Do not overlap chicken pieces.) Or heat grill and place two pieces of chicken in a piece of aluminum foil. Cover chicken with sauce, fold aluminum closed, and cook on grill until done.

3. Serve while still hot. It is possible the yogurt will break down during cooking, but this does not change the taste.

CHICKEN AND CRANBERRIES

It takes a little time to ready everything in this recipe for the oven, but it's worth it. A variation of the classic Russian dish Chicken Kiev, this filling is a lot more healthy and tasty. Serves 3–6, depending on appetite.

6 chicken breasts, boneless, skinless
Onion salt (sprinkle)
16-oz can of whole cranberries
2 Tbl butter or olive oil
1/4 cup fine dry bread crumbs
2 tsp dried parsley flakes
1/2 tsp paprika
1/2 tsp ground ginger
1/4 tsp ground cayenne pepper
1/2 tsp sage

1. Set oven at 350°F (180°C) degrees. Wash and rinse chicken breasts. Pound lightly until reduced to 1/4-inch thickness; sprinkle with onion salt.

2. Put 2 Tbl of cranberries in center of each breast. Tuck in the sides and roll the breast like a jellyroll and secure with a toothpick. Brush the outside with the melted butter or olive oil.

3. In a bowl, combine bread crumbs, sage, parsley, paprika, ginger, and cayenne pepper. Roll each breast in the mixture to coat it. Place the chicken in a shallow baking dish.

4. Bake uncovered for 30–35 minutes, until done.

5. In the meantime, warm the leftover cranberries. Spoon the cranberries over the chicken breast before serving.

6. Goes great with instant stuffing.

SPICY BAKED CHICKEN

This would work as well on a rotisserie, which normally requires too much extra stuff to haul along. Serves 2–4.

1 4-lb whole fryer-broiler
1/4 cup fresh lime juice
3 Tbl olive oil
1 small onion, minced
2 large cloves garlic, minced (2 tsp)
2 tsp oregano leaves
1 tsp salt
1/4 tsp black pepper
2 tsp basil leaves

1. Trim chicken of excess fat.

2. In a large resealable plastic bag, mix lime juice, olive oil, onion, garlic, oregano, basil, salt, and pepper. Add chicken and coat it completely, turning bag and chicken several times.

3. Cook in oven at 350°F (180°C) for 45–50 minutes. Drumsticks should move easily, and juices should be clear.

4. Let stand 10 minutes after cooking. Slice off legs and split breast.

SPICY ORIENTAL BAKED CHICKEN

This cooks well either on the grill or in the oven with indirect heat. Either way, this is an incredibly simple but tasty preparation. Serves 3–4.

1 4-lb whole broiler-fryer
2/3 cups soy sauce (or Worcestershire sauce)
2 tsp wine (white or red wine, or apple cider vinegar)
1 tsp ground ginger
2 garlic cloves, minced (2 tsp)

1. Mix all ingredients and brush mixture over chicken.

2. Cook at 350°F (180°C) for 45–50 minutes, until drumsticks move easily and juices are clear.

3. Let stand for 10 minutes before carving.

SPICY INDIAN BAKED CHICKEN

Unlike many Indian recipes, this one does not require yogurt. Serves 4.

4 skinless chicken breasts
1/3 cup honey
2 Tbl lemon juice
1 tsp sesame oil
1/4 tsp salt
2 Tbl minced garlic
1/2 tsp paprika
1/4 tsp ground cinnamon
1/4 tsp cayenne pepper
1/4 tsp white pepper
1/2 tsp ground cumin

1. Mix all the ingredients together and pour into a resealable bag. Add chicken, coat completely, and let marinate for an hour.

2. Place the chicken in a baking dish lined with foil. Spoon some of the leftover marinade on top. Reserve the rest for basting chicken once it is cooked.

3. Bake at 400°F (200°C) for 30–40 minutes.

GINGER CHICKEN

This recipe, one of my favorites, is worth the price of the book. Anyone who likes the taste of ginger will be fixing this one often. And it's so simple! *The chicken needs to marinate for 30 minutes.*

1 whole chicken (or the equivalent number of pieces)
1 Tbl ground ginger
1 Tbl soy sauce
1/4 cup olive oil

1. Mix ginger, soy sauce, and olive oil in a nonaluminum container or a resealable plastic bag. Marinate the chicken in it for at least half an hour.

2. Bake chicken at 375°F (190°C) for 50–60 minutes, basting frequently with juices and leftover marinade. Let it set for 10 minutes before carving.

JERK BAKED FISH I

This is best done with the fish fillets, although a whole fish also works well. The problem with a whole fish is that it may take considerably longer to cook. This serves 3.

1 lb fish fillets
1 Tbl chopped parsley
1 Tbl lemon juice
1 tsp dry jerk seasoning (see Chapter 4)
3 Tbl olive oil
1 medium onion, sliced
1 Tbl minced garlic
2 Tbl water (or beer or wine)

1. Rub fillets with jerk seasoning, lemon juice, olive oil, minced garlic, and parsley.

2. Place fish in baking dish. Sprinkle with water. Place thin onion slices on top of fillets. Cook, covered, for 30–35 minutes at 350°F (180°C), or until fish flakes with a fork.

JERK BAKED FISH II

This is a much spicier version, for those who truly adore the taste of jerk, as I do. Serves 3.

1 lb fish fillets
1 or 2 Tbl wet jerk seasoning (see Chapter 4)
3 Tbl olive oil
1 Tbl minced garlic

1. Using as much of the wet jerk seasoning as you like, rub the fish with a mix of jerk seasoning, olive oil, and garlic.

2. Bake fish, covered at 350°F (180°C) for 30–35 minutes or until it flakes.

APRICOT-MUSTARD CHICKEN OR FISH

Either fish or chicken can be used for this very tasty recipe, my favorite way to bake fish. Serves 4.

1 lb skinless, boneless chicken breasts or fish fillets
4 Tbl apricot jam
2 Tbl Dijon mustard
1/2 cup Italian bread crumbs
Olive oil or margarine for cooking

1. Mix apricot and mustard together. Rub over both sides of chicken or fish. Sprinkle meat with Italian bread crumbs.

2. In a greased baking dish, place fillets in preheated oven and cook at 350°F (180°C). Fish is done when it flakes, about 20 minutes. Chicken will take 10–15 minutes longer.

ARGENTINE-STYLE STEAK

A delicious way to treat lesser cuts of meat. This goes especially well with mashed potatoes. Serves 4.

1 lb cubed sirloin
1 1/2 cup red wine
1 tsp Worcestershire sauce
2 Tbl flour
1 Tbl sugar
1 Tbl curry powder
1/2 tsp ground ginger
1 Tbl lemon juice
Salt and pepper to taste

1. Dredge meat in flour and place in baking dish. Mix all other ingredients and pour over steak.

2. Bake uncovered at 350°F (180°C) until meat is tender.

SHEPHERD'S PIE

Always a favorite with avid meat-and-potatoes types, since that's all the dish is. I've always thought of this dish as the British version of spaghetti. Serves 4.

1 lb ground beef (or turkey)
1 medium onion, chopped
1 medium green pepper, chopped
1 10 1/2-oz can condensed vegetable soup
Dash of thyme
Dash of salt
1 cup of mashed potatoes

1. Brown beef, onion, and pepper. Drain and discard fat.

2. In a 1-quart baking dish, mix the ground beef, onion, green pepper, soup, thyme, and salt. Spoon mashed potatoes around the top edge of the dish.

3. Cook uncovered for 15 minutes at 425°F (220°C).

BAKED FISH WITH GARLIC

This works well with any firm, white fish, fresh or saltwater. Avoid oily fish, which tend to taste strong. If the fish has been frozen, let it soak in a mix of water (3/4) and lemon juice (1/4) for 10 minutes. It makes all the difference in the world in terms of taste.

1 lb fish fillets
4 Tbl olive oil
1 tsp minced garlic
Dash of oregano

1. Pat fish dry and place in greased cooking dish. Mix olive oil, garlic, and oregano; baste the fish.

2. Bake covered at 350°F (180°C), basting occasionally, for 25–30 minutes, until fish begins to flake.

PICANTE MEATLOAF

This is one of the best meatloafs I've ever tasted. Hope there are leftovers since meatloaf sandwiches are great. Use more picante sauce, BBQ sauce, or mustard for a sandwich topping. Serves 4.

1 lb ground lean hamburger (or turkey)
1/2 cup medium picante sauce
2 eggs
3/4 cup Italian bread crumbs
1 Tbl minced garlic
1 Tbl leaf basil
1 Tbl oregano
2 Tbl prepared mustard
1 onion, chopped
2 Tbl Parmesan cheese (optional)
1 Tbl oregano leaves

1. In an oven dish, mix all ingredients together thoroughly.

2. Bake at 375°F (190°C) for 45 minutes. Allow to cool for several minutes before slicing and serving.

CHAPTER FOURTEEN

Desserts and Breads

You'll need an oven to make many of the desserts on the trail. Realistically, you'll probably want to make these at home and take them with you, since none of them need to be served piping hot. The pies may be out of the question for backpackers, but the trail mixes, cookies, or popcorn won't.

SOUR CREAM FRENCH APPLE COBBLER

The name makes this sound like something loaded with fat, but it's not. Start baking this just as you begin preparing the main course. People will be salivating by the time it comes out of the oven.

1 cup nonfat sour cream
1 egg
1/4 cup sugar
2 tsp lemon juice
2 Tbl flour
3 cups sliced and peeled apples
1 cup raisins
1 Tbl ground cinnamon
1 tsp ground allspice
1 unbaked 9-inch pie shell with top crust

1. Mix everything in a bowl and pour in pastry shell. Seal with the pie crust.

2. Place in the oven and cook at 350°F (180°C) for 50 minutes.

EASY GARLIC BREAD

The title of this chapter says "breads," but in my camp there is only one bread—garlic bread. There are lots of ways to make garlic bread. The best ones emphasize the garlic over the bread. This version can be made crunchy if you leave out the mayonnaise or olive oil, but I've never much liked dry garlic bread that crumbles and falls in your food.

1/2 cup grated Parmesan cheese
1/4 cup nonfat mayonnaise or olive oil (try each sometime!)
4 Tbl minced garlic
3 Tbl chopped oregano leaves
1 loaf French bread, cut lengthwise and into 8 pieces

1. Combine all the ingredients and spread on the cut sides of the bread.

2. If a grill warming rack is available, use it to heat up bread. Or use your accessory for grilling fish, onions, and so on. Or wrap each of 8 pieces in aluminum foil and place on grill, turning frequently. After about 10–15 minutes, unwrap the tops and place the bread facedown on the grill for 1–2 minutes to brown. Be careful not to burn the bread.

BANANAS AND OATS

It makes no difference if the bananas get mashed in your pack, because that's how they're going to end up anyway. You can simplify this recipe even more by peeling the bananas and placing them in a resealable bag before leaving home. Then you won't be scraping mashed banana off the peels. This serves 4.

4 bananas
1/2 cup instant oats
1 1/2 cups chopped walnuts
1 tsp vanilla extract
1/2 tsp nutmeg or 1/2 tsp ground ginger

Peel the bananas and mash everything together. Place on an ungreased cookie sheet and bake for 20 minutes at 350°F (180°C).

BANANA FRITTERS

Another good use for mashed bananas. Can be used as a dessert or an added surprise for breakfast.

2 mashed ripe bananas
1 egg
4 Tbl flour
1 Tbl sugar
1 tsp baking powder
Oil for frying

1. Mix sugar, flour, baking powder, and banana until smooth. Beat egg and fold into mixture.

2. Drop spoonfuls into hot oil and fry until golden brown. Sprinkle with sugar and serve when slightly cooled.

KEY LIME PIE

Guaranteed to be the best you've ever had. It's the real thing, which means it isn't green. Lime juice, like lemon juice, is yellow. The green tint found in many so-called Key lime pies comes from color additives, probably left over from St. Patrick's Day. It's one thing to eat green food when you're partying and everything tastes like beer, quite another when it comes to something really important, like desserts.

Crust
1 1/2 cups graham cracker crumbs
8 Tbl melted butter

Filling
1/3 cup lime juice
1 14-oz can condensed milk
2 egg yolks

Meringue
1/4 tsp cream of tartar
2 egg whites
4 Tbl sugar

1. Mix crust ingredients together, press into 9-inch pie pan, and bake at 350°F (180°C) for 15 minutes.

2. Mix filling ingredients well, and fill pie shell.

3. Beat meringue ingredients until fluffy, put on top of filling. Bake at 325°F (160°C) for 15 minutes.

CHERRY NO-FAT CHEESECAKE

This is not a dessert anyone ever expects to find on a camping trip. One taste and you will be hooked forever.

3 8-oz packages of nonfat cream cheese
1 16-oz can light cherry pie filling
1 tsp vanilla
3 egg whites
1/2 cup sugar
1 Tbl butter or no-fat margarine

1. Let cream cheese sit at room temperature for at least half an hour. In a bowl, beat together cream cheese, vanilla, egg whites, and sugar until smooth.

2. Rub the butter over the bottom of a pie dish. Add cheesecake filling and cook at 325°F (160°C) for 45 minutes.

3. Remove pie from oven and let cool. Top with can of light cherry filling. Refrigerate for at least an hour. For variation, try putting this in a graham cracker pie shell (a high-calorie option).

SINFULLY RICH NO-FAT CHOCOLATE SWIRL CHEESECAKE

Adding chocolate to the Cherry No-Fat Cheesecake was initially tried as an improvement. The taste difference was so striking that the cherries never got added. They simply aren't needed.

3 8-oz packages nonfat cream cheese
6 oz real chocolate chips
1 tsp vanilla
3 egg whites
1/2 cup sugar
1 Tbl butter or no-fat margarine

1. Let cream cheese sit at room temperature for at least 30 minutes. In the meantime, melt chocolate in a double boiler—that is, any container warmed by steam or hot water and not by direct heat.

2. Mix together cream cheese, vanilla, egg whites, and sugar. Grease the bottom of a pie dish with butter. Pour in half the cheesecake batter. Mix the other half of cheesecake batter with the melted chocolate and pour into the pie dish.

3. Cook at 325°F (160°C) for 45 minutes. Refrigerate for one hour before serving. No topping necessary.

SPICY POPCORN

Popcorn is considered one of the better snack/dessert foods. The following ideas will give you enough different ways to fix popcorn for more than a week. These flavors are to be added to 4 cups of popped corn.

Tangy Italian: *1/4 cup Parmesan cheese, a dash of garlic salt, and 1 1/2 Tbl melted butter or margarine.*

Cheesy Corn: *Same recipe as above, but without the garlic salt.*

Tex-Mex: *A pinch of chili powder (hot or mild, you decide) or a pinch of taco seasoning mixed with butter.*

Pizza: *A pinch of parsley, oregano, and basil added to the butter.*

Cinnamon: *Sprinkle with cinnamon sugar, not just plain cinnamon.*

Spicy Hot: *A dash or more of hot sauce with the butter.*

Caramel Corn: *Drizzle with warm caramel sauce.*

Butterscotch Corn: *Drizzle with warm butterscotch sauce.*

TRAIL MIXES

Well, they do taste more like dessert than anything else. You need a dehydrator to make all but the first. Use the ingredients in equal quantities.

Classic Gorp: *Seedless raisins, peanuts, and M&Ms.*

Fruit Cocktail: *Mix dried pineapple, apples, cherries, cranberries, raisins, and bananas.*

Caribbean Crunch: *Dried pineapple, dried papaya, unsweetened coconut flakes, chocolate chips, peanuts, and cashews.*

OATMEAL RAISIN COOKIES

This is the most sugar-packed recipe in the book, and it tastes it. But it is fairly low in fat. Makes about 40 2-inch cookies.

1/4 cup canola oil
1 tsp vanilla
1/2 tsp allspice
3 cups regular or quick oats
1 cup raisins
1 cup all-purpose flour
1 tsp salt
1/2 tsp baking powder
2 large eggs or 1/2 cup fat-free liquid egg substitute
1/2 cup granulated sugar
1 level cup brown sugar

1. In a bowl, mix the oil, allspice, brown sugar, and granulated sugar. Once the sugar starts to dissolve, add egg and vanilla and mix in thoroughly.

2. Add oats, flour, baking powder, and salt and form a soft dough. Add raisins and mix in thoroughly.

3. On a nonstick baking sheet, place 2-inch balls of dough and space cookies about 2 inches apart. Dip your fingers in water to keep dough from sticking to them.

4. Bake at 350°F (180°C) for 12–14 minutes or until golden brown.

Equivalent-Measure and Conversion Charts

The following charts are designed to help you convert one measure to another and to help you estimate how many servings you can count on from ounce, pound, gram, or liter measures.

If you cannot find the measure you are looking for in the left-hand column, try the center or right-hand column, then read backward to see how to convert.

STANDARD AMERICAN MEASURES

Fluid ounces are used for liquid measure; the equivalents in cup and spoon measurements are always the same.

Dry or solid ounces and pounds will vary in cup measurement according to the product.

    3 teaspoons = 1 tablespoon
    2 tablespoons = 1 jigger (small) = 1 fluid ounce
    1 jigger (large) = 3 tablespoons = 1 1/2 fluid ounces
    4 tablespoons = 1/4 cup = 2 fluid ounces
    5 1/2 tablespoons = 1/3 cup
    8 tablespoons = 1/2 cup = 4 fluid ounces
    11 tablespoons = 2/3 cup
    16 tablespoons = 1 cup = 8 fluid ounces
    1 1/2 cups = 12 fluid ounces
    8 ounces (dry) = 1/2 pound
    16 ounces (dry) = 1 pound
    2 cups = 1 pint = 16 fluid ounces
    2 pints (4 cups) = 1 quart = 32 fluid ounces
    1 fifth of wine = 1/5 gallon = 25 fluid ounces
    8 cups = 1/2 gallon = 64 fluid ounces
    4 quarts (16 cups) = 1 gallon = 128 fluid ounces
    8 quarts (dry) = 1 peck = 32 cups
    4 pecks (dry) = 1 bushel

BRITISH MEASURES

1 tablespoon English = 4 teaspoons American (1 1/3 American tablespoons)
Dessertspoon (English) = 1 tablespoon American
1 cup English (1/2 pint) = 1 1/4 cups American
1 pint imperial = 20 fluid ounces = 2 1/2 cups American
1 gill = 1/2 cup American plus 2 American tablespoons
1 gallon imperial = 160 fluid ounces = 5 quarts = 20 cups

GRAM-LITER TABLES

Dry-Solid Measures

Ounces	Convenient Equivalent	Grams
.035 oz	1 g	1 g
1 oz	30 g	28.35 g
2 oz	60 g	56.7 g
3 oz	85 g	85.05 g
4 oz	115 g	113.4 g
5 oz	140 g	141.7 g
6 oz	180 g	170.1 g
8 oz	225 g	226.8 g
9 oz	250 g	255.1 g
10 oz	285 g	283.5 g
12 oz	340 g	340.2 g
14 oz	400 g	396.9 g
16 oz	450 g	453.6 g
20 oz	560 g	566.99 g
24 oz	675 g	680.4 g

Liquid Measures

Cups	Spoons	Liquid Ounces	Milliliters
	1 tsp	1/6 oz	5 mL
	1 Tbl	1/2 oz	15 mL
1/4 c	4 Tbl	2 oz	59 mL
1/3 c	5 Tbl	2 2/3 oz	79 mL
1/2 c		4 oz	119 mL
2/3 c		5 1/3 oz	157 mL
3/4 c		6 oz	178 mL
1 c		8 oz	237 mL

FOOD EQUIVALENTS

1 cup of:	Ounces	Grams
granulated sugar	6 1/2 ounces	185 g
icing sugar	5 ounces	150 g
flour	4 ounces	120 g
raisins	5 ounces	150 g
rolled oats	3 ounces	85 g
chopped walnuts	3 ounces	85 g
soft bread crumbs	3 ounces	85 g
grated cheese	4 ounces	120 g

Flour, Corn Flour, Cocoa, Custard Powder
1 rounded tsp = 1/4 oz = 7.5 g
1 level Tbl = 1/2oz = 15 g
1 rounded Tbl = 1 oz = 30 g
1 teacup = 3 oz = 85 g

Sugar, Rice, Lentils
1 level Tbl = 1 oz = 30 g
1 teacup = 6 oz = 170 g
1 bkfst cup = 8 oz = 230 g

Warmed Syrup
1 level Tbl = 1 oz = 30 g

Bread/Cake Crumbs
1 heaping cup = 1/2 oz = 15 g

Liquids
1 teacup = 1/3 pt = 190 mL
1 bkfst cup = 1/2 pt = 250 mL

Butter
1 Tbl = 1/2 oz = 15 g

DIMENSIONS OF BAKING PANS, TINS, ETC.

Inches	mm	cm
1	25	2.5
5	125	12.5
6	150	15
8	200	20
9	230	23
12	300	30

OVEN TEMPERATURES

Oven Temp.	Fahrenheit (°F)	Celsius (°C)	Gas
Very Cool	200	95	1
Cool	250	120	2
Moderate	350	180	3
Moderately Hot	375	190	4
Hot	425	220	5–6
Very Hot	500	260	7+